IMPROVISATION STARTERS

REVISED AND EXPANDED

WRITER'S DIGEST
BOOKS

WritersDigest.com
Cincinnati, Ohio

IMPROVISATION STARTERS

STARTERS

REVISED AND EXPANDED

More Than 1,000 Improvisation Scenarios
for the Theater and Classroom

PHILIP BERNARDI

For more resources for writers, visit www.writersdigest.com.

20 19 18 17 16   5 4 3 2 1

Distributed in Canada by Fraser Direct
100 Armstrong Avenue
Georgetown, Ontario, Canada L7G 5S4
Tel: (905) 877-4411

Distributed in the U.K. and Europe by F+W Media International
Brunel House, Newton Abbot, Devon, TQ12 4PU, England
Tel: (+44) 1626-323200, Fax: (+44) 1626-323319
E-mail: postmaster@davidandcharles.co.uk

ISBN-13: 978-1-4403-4754-2

Edited by Chelsea Plunkett
Designed by Alexis Estoye
Production coordinated by Debbie Thomas

DEDICATION

To Carol, always and forever

ACKNOWLEDGMENTS

I wish to thank my wife, Carol Bernardi, for her continued love, understanding, and patience as I wrote this new edition of *Improvisation Starters*; my sister, Diane Havens, for the inspiration; my brothers, Alfred Bernardi and Thomas Bernardi, for their support; my mother and father for encouraging my passion for the performing arts; Beth Manzella for the e-mail exchanges; Ashley Kromrey for her help in promoting my work; my former colleagues and students in the Pascack Valley Regional High School District for giving me the opportunity to try out many of the scenarios included in this edition; my new colleagues and students at Immaculate Heart Academy for welcoming me with warmth and kindness; the outstanding editorial, design, and sales teams at F+W Media for their diligence in the production of this book, with special thanks to Chelsea Plunkett for her invaluable feedback and suggestions; and teachers, students, and performers everywhere for using the first edition in their classrooms and studios and wanting more.

ABOUT THE AUTHOR

 Philip Bernardi taught theater, video production, journalism, English, and speech communication in the Pascack Valley Regional High School District in Montvale, New Jersey, for thirty-eight years, and also directed more than fifty musical and drama productions for the district. Presently, he's a communications teacher and production coordinator at Immaculate Heart Academy in Washington Township, New Jersey. Mr. Bernardi holds a B.A. in speech and theater and an M.A. in theater from Montclair State University in Upper Montclair, New Jersey. He has also run a series of workshops for non-theater teachers called "Using Improvisation in the Non-Theater Classroom." Outside of the classroom, he enjoys playing acoustic guitar and singing in restaurants and pubs near his home in Mahwah, New Jersey, where he lives with his wife, Carol, and two Bichon Frise dogs, Monty and Daisy.

TABLE OF CONTENTS

INTRODUCTION

Imagine if our lives were scripted. We'd wake up each morning knowing exactly what we'd say to the people we met, and in addition, we'd know exactly how they would respond. We'd know when we needed to be happy, sad, angry, calm, excited, afraid, nervous, confused, etc., as well as why we were supposed to feel that way. We'd even know when to stand, when to sit down, and when to move to another location.

Life would be pretty dull. We'd have no reason to actually listen to anyone since we'd already know what everyone had to say. We couldn't make any decisions for ourselves because all our decisions would have already been made for us. We'd have no choice in who to love or hate or when to laugh or cry. We'd have no honest thoughts, no instincts to trust, no personal beliefs, no confidence in ourselves, nothing to be excited about.

Thankfully, our lives are not scripted. Each day we wake up not knowing precisely how the day will turn out. We never know when we might meet new people and what we might say to them or what they will say to us in return. We are free to change our moods and feelings at any given moment. Something could happen in an instant that could change the entire direction of our lives.

In a way, life is like one long improvisation. We can prepare for what lies ahead, but we can never be completely sure that things will turn out as we plan. This is what makes life interesting. We just never know for certain what each moment will bring.

This revised and expanded edition of *Improvisation Starters* includes more than one thousand new scenarios, each designed to begin an improvised scene. It's important to remember that the situations included just provide a way to *start* the scene. How it develops and eventually ends will depend largely on the imagination and creativity of the performers.

Actors need to make it easy for their audiences to willingly suspend their disbelief, and improvisation is a great way for an actor to practice bringing spontaneity, honesty, insight, excitement, and energy to the stage or set, and make the audience accept they are watching real life. But improvisation is not just an effective tool for actors; it's also a great way to help anyone think critically, build self-confidence, communicate clearly, and develop valuable interpersonal skills. With this in mind, a section on how teachers of subjects other than theater can use improvisation in their classes is included in this edition.

Of course, improvisation is more than a method of improvement. It is an art form in itself that can and should be enjoyed and appreciated for its own entertainment value.

Happy improvising!

USING CHARACTER CONFLICTS

Life is filled with conflict. We may try to escape it, but sometimes conflict is unavoidable, especially when the other people involved have agendas completely different from our own. It's in those situations that we must find a resolution in order to accomplish our objectives.

A strong conflict can provide the foundation for an excellent improvisation. This chapter contains two hundred scenarios that include characters with conflicting beliefs, motivations, wants, or needs. Situations are provided for two or three players, but many of the situations for two players may be adjusted to involve three or more.

The instructor should conduct the improvisations in the following way:

- Ask the players to take the stage or playing area. The stage or playing area should be bare, except for two or three chairs and possibly a small table the players may wish to use during the improvisation.
- Assign each player a role, and read the improvisation situation aloud to both the players and the audience.
- Immediately after doing this, provide each player with the background information given for his or her individual role. This should be done by whispering it to each player privately. *It is important that the players do not know in advance the back-*

ground information provided for the other character or characters in the scene.

Before beginning, review the following guidelines with your players:

- Develop a strong character objective before you begin the scene, and keep it in mind during the improvisation. Everything you say or do must be directed toward accomplishing that objective. If you find what you're saying or doing to accomplish your objective is not working, then try something else. However, the objective itself should not be changed. Your objective provides the energy and focus necessary to keep the scene moving.
- Focus only on the other actor(s), not the audience. All outward expression should result from an honest reaction to the situation, not from what you think the audience should be seeing. Don't play emotions; just become involved in the situation. Don't try to be "dramatic." You're not writing a play, you're simply trying to reach your objective.
- Go along with any new element introduced by your partner. If your partner says he is married, don't question it (unless, of course, you believe he is lying).
- Pantomime the use of any props that may be necessary.
- Continue trying to accomplish your objective until the instructor tells you to stop. Remember: If you think you're getting nowhere with one line of action, try another.

After each improvisation, you may wish to discuss the performance with your players and the audience. You may use the following questions to guide your discussion:

- How closely did the players stick to their objectives?
- What specific strategies did the players use to try to accomplish their objectives? What specific actions did the players choose to carry out those strategies? Did each player use an original or creative approach?

- Did the players do anything that seemed phony or contrived? Were any guilty of playing to the audience instead of to each other?
- Did any character element seem to be stereotyped?
- Did any of the players break concentration during the scene?
- Was there too much talk and too little action?
- Did the players use their imaginations well?

IMPORTANT NOTE: Unless a specific gender is required, the roles described in the following improvisation situations may be played by either males or females. You may replace *he* with *she*, *man* with *woman*, *girl* with *boy*, *daughter* with *son*, etc.

School Days

Two Players

1. THE SITUATION: A girl meets a boy in a hallway of their high school. The week before, the girl had accepted the boy's invitation to their senior prom.

>**GIRL:** You accepted this boy's invitation only because the guy you really wanted to go with didn't ask you. Yesterday, the boy you were hoping would ask you finally did … and you said yes! Now you need to find a way to tell this boy you no longer want to go to the prom with him.
>
>**BOY:** You're very excited about going to the prom with this girl.

2. THE SITUATION: A high school principal sees a student sitting on a bench outside the school in the middle of a class period.

>**STUDENT:** Earlier, you asked your teacher for permission to go to the restroom. You actually just wanted to take a break from the class because you were becoming bored.
>
>**PRINCIPAL:** You're wondering why this student is sitting on a bench outside the school instead of sitting in his class.

3. THE SITUATION: A Spanish teacher pulls aside one of his students just after the class period ends.

TEACHER: You're wondering why this student's grades have suddenly started to decline.

STUDENT: You've decided you no longer care about learning Spanish since you figure most people in the world today can speak English.

4. THE SITUATION: A teacher notices a student sending a text message during class.

STUDENT: You know the teacher has a "no texts in class" policy, but you desperately need to get a message to your friend about a change in your after-school plans.

TEACHER: You don't allow texting in your class at all—no exceptions!

5. THE SITUATION: A student asks his teacher if he may be excused to go to the bathroom.

TEACHER: Last week, you gave this student permission to go to the bathroom but later discovered he met his friends in the cafeteria and never went to the bathroom.

STUDENT: You have to use the bathroom badly!

6. THE SITUATION: A student tutors another student in math.

TUTOR: This student's mother is paying you a lot of money to tutor her daughter and expects results, so you want the student to focus on what you're teaching her.

STUDENT: You hate math, and you're refusing to cooperate with the tutor.

7. THE SITUATION: A teacher reprimands a student for arriving late to class.

TEACHER: You insist that all students get to your class on time, and you're not interested in listening to excuses.

STUDENT: You found out that today is the teacher's birthday, and you wanted to surprise her with a present. Before class, you were shopping for the gift. You're late because you lost track of time while looking for the perfect thing. You have the gift with you.

8. THE SITUATION: A student asks her friend why she wrote a terrible review of her performance in a play for the school newspaper.

> **FIRST STUDENT:** You can't believe your friend wrote such awful things about you in the school paper.
>
> **STUDENT REVIEWER:** You feel bad about writing such negative things about your friend's performance, but you feel that as a reporter, you need to be honest and unbiased.

9. THE SITUATION: A girl asks her friend if she would like to sing a duet with her at an upcoming high school talent show.

> **FIRST GIRL:** You know your friend doesn't have a particularly good singing voice, but you think she needs a boost of confidence. You're not concerned about sounding bad; you just want to help your friend feel good about herself.
>
> **SECOND GIRL:** You're surprised that your friend has asked you to sing at the talent show with her. You love to sing, but you know you don't sing very well. You'd love to do it, but you also don't want to make a fool of yourself.

10. THE SITUATION: A teacher criticizes a student's poorly prepared oral presentation.

> **TEACHER:** You are tired of listening to poorly prepared presentations from students whom you believe are lazy and unmotivated.
>
> **STUDENT:** You put a great deal of work into this presentation and believe you've done a great job with it.

11. THE SITUATION: A high school soccer player meets with his coach to discuss his participation in the sport.

> **SOCCER PLAYER:** Even though you're a very talented soccer player, you want to quit the team so you can spend more time playing and practicing guitar, which is your first love.

COACH: This student is unquestionably your best player and is key to the team's success.

12. THE SITUATION: A high school senior class valedictorian discusses his post-graduation plans with his guidance counselor.

VALEDICTORIAN: You're not interested in going to college. You've been interested in auto mechanics your entire life and want to start working as an auto mechanic immediately after high school.

GUIDANCE COUNSELOR: Even though you have no problem with someone choosing auto mechanics as a career, you believe this particular student would be making a mistake by not attending college.

13. THE SITUATION: The director of a school play tells the lead role's understudy he must play the role in tonight's performance.

DIRECTOR: The show can't go on unless the understudy plays the part in tonight's performance. You are fully confident the understudy will do a great job.

UNDERSTUDY: Although you are excited about having the opportunity to play the part, you're scared to death at the thought of doing it.

14. THE SITUATION: A student asks his friend why he's come to school dressed in a suit and tie.

STUDENT: Students in your school normally dress very casually; you're wondering why your friend is dressed in formal attire today.

FRIEND: You've decided to reinvent yourself by coming to school in a suit and tie for the rest of the year.

15. THE SITUATION: A male student in a class filled solely with boys asks his teacher to recommend his transfer to another English class.

STUDENT: You don't have a problem with the teacher or any of the other students in the class. You'd just rather be in a class that has a few girls in it.

TEACHER: You can't recommend a transfer just because the student wants to be in a class with some girls in it.

16. THE SITUATION: A student tries to convince his friend to skip school for the day.

> **FIRST STUDENT:** You have a plan for skipping school without getting caught, but you need your friend's help to pull it off.
>
> **SECOND STUDENT:** You'd love to skip school for the day, but you're not so sure your friend's plan will work.

17. THE SITUATION: A high school teacher tells a student he accidentally dented the student's car in the parking lot and offers to pay for the damage.

> **TEACHER:** When you were getting out of your car, your door hit the fender of the student's car and created a small dent.
>
> **STUDENT:** You have a proposal for the teacher: He doesn't have to pay for the damage if he exempts you from doing homework for the next three weeks.

18. THE SITUATION: The wrestling team coach tells one of his wrestlers he's scheduled to face a female opponent at this afternoon's match.

> **COACH:** The female wrestler is one of the best wrestlers in the state, and you want all your wrestlers to take her very seriously.
>
> **WRESTLER:** You have a huge ego and can't imagine any female could beat you in a wrestling match.

19. THE SITUATION: A student tells his physical education teacher he can't participate in gym class today because he has a back injury.

> **STUDENT:** Your back is fine, but you're feeling lazy and don't want to participate in today's gym class.
>
> **TEACHER:** You don't believe this student has a back injury.

20. THE SITUATION: A student asks his teacher why he doesn't allow students to eat in class when the teacher often eats in class himself.

STUDENT: You think the teacher is a hypocrite, and you intend to let him know.

TEACHER: Your response to the student is "Do as I say, not as I do." You don't owe him or any other student an explanation.

21. THE SITUATION: A teacher tries to calm a nervous student who sees a bee flying around the classroom.

STUDENT: You are allergic to bees and fear being stung; you want the teacher to kill the bee.

TEACHER: You try to relax the student by telling him the best strategy is to simply ignore the bee.

22. THE SITUATION: A high school senior student asks his social studies teacher to write him a college recommendation.

STUDENT: You know your grades in social studies are poor, but they're better than your grades in any other class. You've been slacking off this year as a senior, but you still want to go to college and need to include teacher recommendations with your college applications.

TEACHER: This student has done little work for you so far this year, and you have nothing positive to say about him. You're surprised he even approached you about a recommendation.

23. THE SITUATION: The captain of a high school chess team asks the school principal to consider organizing a pep rally for the team's upcoming tournament.

CHESS TEAM CAPTAIN: The school has pep rallies for its sports teams, and you think it's only fair to also have pep rallies for its nonsports teams.

PRINCIPAL: You've never considered having a pep rally in support of any school club or team except sports teams. You just don't believe a pep rally for the chess team would go over well with the student body.

24. THE SITUATION: A teacher attempts to gain the attention of a sleepy student.

> **STUDENT:** You were up late last night finishing a research paper that is due today, and you're struggling to stay awake in this morning's class.
>
> **TEACHER:** You resent that the student is falling asleep in your class.

25. THE SITUATION: A student speaks loudly to her friend in a quiet library.

> **FIRST STUDENT:** You're trying to speak softly, but you're one of those people who just can't whisper.
>
> **SECOND STUDENT:** You're embarrassed by your friend's loud voice. Everyone around you is staring at you both.

26. THE SITUATION: A student informs her English teacher that she aspires to become a novelist.

> **STUDENT:** You love this teacher's English class. It inspired your desire to become a novelist, and you'd like to share your passion for writing with your teacher.
>
> **TEACHER:** This student has always worked hard in your class, and because of that, you admire her. However, you don't think she is talented enough to become a novelist. You don't believe in giving any student false encouragement.

27. THE SITUATION: A student football player informs his coach that he's quitting the team because he's afraid of brain injury.

> **PLAYER:** Yesterday you read an article in the newspaper about the dangers of suffering permanent brain injury from playing high school football.
>
> **COACH:** This student is your best player; the team will be considerably weaker without him.

28. THE SITUATION: An English teacher questions a student about a paper on *The Great Gatsby* that he submitted.

STUDENT: You didn't read the novel. You saw a film version and based your paper on what you saw in the film, even though you were required to read the book before writing the paper.

TEACHER: Many of the references in the paper were included in the latest movie version of *The Great Gatsby* but not the novel. Students were required to read the book before writing the paper.

29. THE SITUATION: A teacher questions one of her brighter students about why her grades have recently been declining.

STUDENT: This teacher had always praised you for your previously excellent work, but other students have teased you for being the teacher's favorite. You're hoping your classmates will stop teasing you if you start producing inferior work.

TEACHER: You know that this student is capable of producing much better work.

30. THE SITUATION: A teacher tells his student to stop filming him during class.

STUDENT: You'd like to watch the video later while preparing for a test on the material the teacher is presenting. You think filming the teacher is easier and better than taking notes.

TEACHER: You don't feel comfortable being filmed during class.

Three Players

31. THE SITUATION: A student stops two other students in the hallway to discuss the food that's served in the school cafeteria.

FIRST STUDENT: You believe food that is high in fat and sugar content should be banned from the cafeteria, and you want the two students to sign a petition that demands healthier food selections.

SECOND STUDENT: You think the food selection in the cafeteria is just fine. You believe all students have the right to eat whatever they like.

THIRD STUDENT: You've never thought much about the food sold in the cafeteria.

32. **THE SITUATION:** A high school student begins pushing, shoving, and mocking another student, when a third intervenes.

FIRST STUDENT: You are bullying another student with the intention of humiliating him.

SECOND STUDENT: You fear the student who is bullying you and feel defenseless.

THIRD STUDENT: You are disgusted by the bully's actions and come to the victim's aid.

33. **THE SITUATION:** Two members of the cheerleading squad speak to the school principal about cheering at girls' basketball games as well as the boys' basketball games.

CHEERLEADERS: You think it's wrong to prohibit cheerleaders from cheering at the girls' games.

PRINCIPAL: Although you agree with the cheerleaders, your hands are tied because school board policy states that cheerleaders may only cheer for the boys' team.

34. **THE SITUATION:** An English teacher praises a student for his outstanding grade on a composition, but another student announces the paper is plagiarized.

TEACHER: You're not sure whether or not to believe the protesting student's accusation.

STUDENT: You wrote this paper on your own and resent your fellow student's accusation.

ACCUSER: You read an almost identical composition online, and you're convinced the student copied and pasted it from the Internet.

35. THE SITUATION: Three students are involved in a food fight in the cafeteria.

> **FIRST STUDENT:** You threw a french fry at your friend, but missed and hit another unsuspecting student.
>
> **SECOND STUDENT:** Your friend tossed a french fry at your face, but you managed to avoid it.
>
> **THIRD STUDENT:** You were eating your lunch, minding your own business, when a french fry thrown by a student on the other side of your lunch table hit you on the back of the head.

36. THE SITUATION: A teacher notices two students flashing hand signals to each other during a class test.

> **TEACHER:** Thinking the students are signaling answers to each other, you accuse them of cheating.
>
> **STUDENTS:** Your hand signals have nothing to do with the test. You're just trying to agree on a time to meet up after school.

37. THE SITUATION: A teacher is about to return two students' tests.

> **STUDENTS:** You both think you scored extremely well on the test and argue about who received the higher grade.
>
> **TEACHER:** You're disappointed in both students; they each failed miserably.

38. THE SITUATION: Two high-school boys attempt to impress a cute new girl.

> **BOYS:** You're each trying desperately to make a positive impression on this girl in the hope that she will agree to go on a date with you.
>
> **GIRL:** You're not interested in either one of these boys; you just want to settle into your new school.

39. THE SITUATION: A high school principal meets with a student and his teacher about a problem between the two. The student claims the teacher is unfairly critical of him.

STUDENT: The teacher constantly tells you that you're lazy and unmotivated.

TEACHER: You don't think you're being unfairly critical; you maintain that you're trying to motivate the student to realize his full potential.

PRINCIPAL: You listen with an open mind to what both the student and teacher have to say.

40. **THE SITUATION:** Two high school friends ask a third to offer her opinion on which of the two is dressed better.

TWO FRIENDS: You've always been very competitive with each other when it comes to the way you dress.

THIRD FRIEND: You don't like how either one is dressed; you think you dress better than both of them.

All in a Day's Work

Two Players

1. **THE SITUATION:** A bartender listens to a customer's complaint about his margarita.

BARTENDER: You believe you are a great bartender and all your drinks are perfect.

PATRON: You think the margarita is too sweet and weak.

2. **THE SITUATION:** A man walks into his apartment and sees his cleaning woman sitting and reading the paper.

MAN: Looking around your apartment, it appears your cleaning woman hasn't cleaned a thing.

CLEANING WOMAN: The apartment appeared to be pretty clean when you arrived earlier, so you thought you'd just do nothing and relax today.

3. **THE SITUATION:** A dental patient feels that his teeth are too white and asks his dentist if anything can be done about it.

PATIENT: You are very self-conscious about your teeth; you think they are much too white.

DENTIST: You think there's nothing wrong with the color of this patient's teeth. In fact, you think they look great.

4. THE SITUATION: A restaurant chef starts to cry when a customer tells him she didn't like her meal.

CHEF: You take it very personally whenever someone complains about a dish you've prepared.

CUSTOMER: Even though you hated the meal, you feel awful about making the chef cry.

5. THE SITUATION: A blind man shows up for a driving lesson.

DRIVING INSTRUCTOR: You're obviously taken aback when you see that your driving student is blind.

BLIND MAN: You're only pretending to be blind. A friend of the driving instructor asked you to play a prank on him.

6. THE SITUATION: A customer browsing in an antique store sees a Chippendale-style chair supposedly made in 1750 and tells the store owner it's a fake.

CUSTOMER: You know quite a bit about vintage American furniture and can easily identify a fake when you see one.

OWNER: You know the chair is a fake, but you've been hoping to sell it to an unsuspecting customer for an outrageous price.

7. THE SITUATION: A newspaper restaurant reviewer asks her editor for an assignment to review her parents' restaurant.

EDITOR: You're reluctant to give her this assignment. Obviously, you don't think she can impartially review her own parents' restaurant.

REVIEWER: You're angry with your parents because they refused to take you in as a partner. You want to get back at them by writing a scathing review of their restaurant.

8. THE SITUATION: A customer in a clothing store attempts to return a dress that was purchased a week ago.

> **CUSTOMER:** You wore this dress to a party a few days ago, but you've decided you don't like it. Even though you know the store has a policy stating that items cannot be returned once they are worn outside the store, you intend to tell the salesperson you never wore the dress.
>
> **SALESPERSON:** The dress this customer wants to return has a stain on it. Clearly, it was worn outside the store, so it is not eligible for return.

9. THE SITUATION: A customer in a restaurant explains to his server that he doesn't have enough money to leave a tip.

> **CUSTOMER:** You feel awful about the fact that you can't leave a tip. You think the server did a great job, and you will return tomorrow with some cash for her.
>
> **SERVER:** You don't believe the customer is short on money. You think he didn't like your service.

10. THE SITUATION: A guy in his thirties asks his dermatologist to do something to the skin on his face to *cause* acne.

> **GUY:** You want a few pimples on your face because you think it will make you look younger.
>
> **DERMATOLOGIST:** This is the strangest request you've ever received from a patient. Dermatologists *treat* acne; they don't *cause* it.

11. THE SITUATION: An office worker speaks to his boss about an e-mail he sent him earlier in the day.

> **OFFICE WORKER:** You sent a group e-mail complaining about your boss to everyone on the staff, not realizing until just after you sent it that your boss would also receive it.
>
> **BOSS:** It's obvious the worker mistakenly included you in a group e-mail sent to the entire staff because it contained

a list of complaints about you. You're a reasonable person, and you realize some of the criticisms are legitimate.

12. THE SITUATION: A customer in a clothing store wants to buy a salesman's jacket, which is lying behind the sales counter.

>**CUSTOMER:** You don't believe the jacket belongs to the salesman; you suspect he's holding it for a friend.

>**SALESMAN:** The customer seems to believe your jacket is for sale, but it isn't.

13. THE SITUATION: A bank manager is about to fire the bank's receptionist because he noticed a tattoo on her neck. The bank has a strict "no tattoo" policy.

>**RECEPTIONIST:** What appears to be a tattoo on your neck is actually a birthmark.

>**BANK MANAGER:** You have little tolerance for workers who break the rules, and you don't accept excuses from anyone.

14. THE SITUATION: An office manager pretends to be talking on his phone to avoid speaking to an employee, when suddenly the phone that he's holding rings!

>**OFFICE MANAGER:** You've been avoiding this employee for days because you know he wants to talk to you about a raise.

>**EMPLOYEE:** You've been trying to speak to your boss about a raise for quite some time. You realize he is faking a phone conversation to avoid you.

15. THE SITUATION: A woman speaks to a construction site foreman about working for him.

>**WOMAN:** You know you have the skills needed to perform well as a construction worker.

>**FOREMAN:** You believe construction work is not for women.

16. THE SITUATION: A woman confronts a young man in the parking lot of a pizza shop.

WOMAN: You recognize this young man as an employee of the pizza shop. Yesterday you ordered a takeout pizza from him. You ordered it with mushrooms, but when you got home, you saw that it had pepperoni on it instead. You were very unhappy about it.

YOUNG MAN: You work as a salesman in the shoe store across the street from the pizza shop. Your lunch break has ended, and you're just leaving the pizza shop to go back to work after enjoying a slice. You have no idea who this woman is.

17. THE SITUATION: A woman on a job interview responds to a question about an item on her résumé.

WOMAN: You are a bit nervous because in an attempt to impress the interviewer, you stated on your résumé that you enjoy reading and that *War and Peace* is your favorite novel. You have never read it.

INTERVIEWER: *War and Peace* is listed on this woman's résumé as her favorite novel. You suspect this isn't true and she just listed it to impress you.

18. THE SITUATION: A male employer calls a female employee into his office to inform her that she's being terminated.

EMPLOYER: This woman is a good worker, but you need to fire her because she looks too much like your ex-wife, whom you hate with a passion. You believe in being completely upfront with your employees and intend to tell her the truth about why you must fire her.

WOMAN: You've been an excellent employee. You've always received great reviews, and you don't understand why you're being fired.

19. THE SITUATION: A restaurant customer complains to his server about the cheeseburger he ordered.

CUSTOMER: You're angry because the slice of cheese was placed under the burger instead of the top. You insist that this affects the taste of the cheeseburger, and you'd like one that is properly made.

SERVER: You know it's important to keep your customers happy and satisfied, but you also feel that customers must have a reasonable complaint before food is sent back to the kitchen and replaced.

20. THE SITUATION: A customer in a hardware store asks a salesman where he can find a roll of *duck* tape.

> **SALESMAN:** You assume the customer means *duct* tape and politely correct him.
>
> **CUSTOMER:** You are sure that the correct name for what you want is *duck* tape, not *duct* tape.

21. THE SITUATION: The owner of a restaurant meets with one of his managers.

> **OWNER:** You need the manager to take on some additional job responsibilities. You realize he should be compensated for the extra work, but unfortunately, you can't afford to give him a raise.
>
> **MANAGER:** You enjoy working in the restaurant, but you feel you don't get paid enough for all you're expected to do.

22. THE SITUATION: A customer in a drugstore asks a pharmacist about a suspicious-looking mole on his neck.

> **PHARMACIST:** You're a pharmacist, not a doctor. You believe the customer needs to be examined by a dermatologist.
>
> **CUSTOMER:** You think pharmacists have enough medical knowledge to diagnose skin ailments, and you'd like to save a few dollars by avoiding a visit to the doctor.

23. THE SITUATION: A trombone player explains to his orchestra director that he can't perform in tonight's concert.

TROMBONE PLAYER: You have a painful pimple on your upper lip; it hurts when you try to play the trombone.

ORCHESTRA DIRECTOR: Your trombonist is a key member of your orchestra, and you don't have a replacement available.

24. **THE SITUATION:** A customer walks inside a grocery store to return extra change the cashier mistakenly gave him earlier that day.

CUSTOMER: You hadn't noticed until you left the store that you were given ten dollars extra change, and you want to return the money. You don't believe in keeping anything that isn't rightfully yours.

CASHIER: You are so impressed by this customer's honesty that you don't want to take back the extra change and insist on making up the difference yourself.

25. **THE SITUATION:** On her first day on the job, a nurse wants to take a selfie with her first patient.

NURSE: You're very excited and proud to have a new job as a nurse, and you want to have a photo of you and your first patient to show your family and friends.

PATIENT: You're in a great deal of pain, and you want the nurse to give you something to relieve it. You think it's absurd that your nurse seems to be more concerned about taking a selfie with you than with your pain.

26. **THE SITUATION:** The owner of a dollar store tells his store manager he intends to raise the price of every item in the store by fifty cents.

OWNER: You're not happy with your low profit margin, and you want the manager to place new price tags on everything in the store.

MANAGER: The owner doesn't seem to realize he owns a *dollar* store. You don't want to get fired, but you need to find a way to tell him that all items in a dollar store should only cost one dollar.

27. THE SITUATION: A restaurant customer asks his server for a slice of cherry pie … but *without* cherries.

> **CUSTOMER:** You're a notorious prankster, and you placed this absurd order just to see how the server responds.
> **SERVER:** This is the strangest request you've ever heard, but you don't want to insult the customer by telling him that.

28. THE SITUATION: A restaurant manager discusses an online review of the restaurant with one of his servers.

> **MANAGER:** The online review includes harsh criticism of this server, and you feel he needs to be doing a better job.
> **WAITER:** You think you're an excellent waiter, and you maintain that if a customer has a problem with you, they should go to a different restaurant.

29. THE SITUATION: The head teller in a bank speaks to the bank manager about a recently posted opening for an assistant bank manager.

> **TELLER:** You've been working at this bank as head teller for ten years now. You're very good at your job and believe you deserve this promotion.
> **BANK MANAGER:** The bank teller is your best employee, and you know he is certainly qualified for the assistant manager position. However, you don't want to offer him the job because you don't think you can find anyone as good to replace him.

30. THE SITUATION: A customer in a restaurant asks the waiter to recommend something to order.

> **CUSTOMER:** Everything on the menu looks great, but you're having trouble deciding what to order.
> **WAITER:** Earlier, the manager told you today would be your last day working at this restaurant. He's sorry, but they need to cut back on staff. You're angry about your dismissal and

tell the customer that everything on the menu is unhealthy, poorly prepared, and overpriced.

Three Players

31. THE SITUATION: Two office workers talk to their boss about the uncomfortably high temperature in the office.

> **FIRST OFFICE WORKER:** You're sweating profusely and want the boss to turn on the air conditioner.
>
> **SECOND OFFICE WORKER:** You are hot and uncomfortable, but you know your boss is a cheapskate and hates to turn on the air conditioning because of the cost. You pretend you're fine with the temperature because you don't want to anger the boss.
>
> **BOSS:** You think the temperature is just fine; you intend to keep the air conditioner off.

32. THE SITUATION: A boss is about to dismiss one of his employees for drinking on the job, when a co-worker comes to his defense.

> **BOSS:** Earlier in the day, you smelled whiskey in the employee's coffee mug. This is all the proof you need to fire him. You don't care what he or anyone else has to say about it.
>
> **EMPLOYEE:** You can't believe you're being fired for drinking on the job. You don't even drink!
>
> **CO-WORKER:** You know your co-worker doesn't drink. You thought it would be funny if you put some whiskey in his coffee cup and watched his expression when he took a sip, but now you feel bad that he's being fired.

33. THE SITUATION: After returning from a party at 4 A.M., a husband and wife speak to their babysitter, who expected them to be home by midnight.

> **HUSBAND:** You don't remember telling the babysitter you'd be home by midnight, so you don't feel obligated to offer the babysitter extra money.

WIFE: You told the babysitter you'd be home by midnight, but you didn't share that information with your husband.

BABYSITTER: You're angry that you had to work an extra four hours, and you want to be compensated for the time.

34. THE SITUATION: An office worker criticizes the work habits of the boss to a co-worker. The boss is standing unnoticed behind them.

WORKER: You maintain that the boss is incompetent and lazy and express your opinion loudly and clearly to your co-worker.

CO-WORKER: In the middle of your co-worker's tirade, you notice the boss standing behind him. You don't particularly like your co-worker, so you encourage him to ramble on, hoping the boss will hear him and fire him.

BOSS: You are amused by what the worker is saying and wait a while before letting him know you are standing directly behind him.

35. THE SITUATION: A boss discovers that two of his employees are dating and tells them that they must break up. The company has a policy that prohibits employees from dating each other.

BOSS: You feel bad about telling this couple they must break up, but you will have no choice but to fire them unless they do.

EMPLOYEES: You're not dating each other; you're just friends.

36. THE SITUATION: A mother and daughter ask the salesperson in a bridal shop for her opinion on the look and fit of the wedding gown the daughter is wearing. The mother has agreed to pay the cost of the gown.

MOTHER: You love this gown and want to buy it for your daughter.

DAUGHTER: You hate this gown and want to try on a different one.

SALESPERSON: You don't like the look and fit of the gown and have nothing positive to say about it. However, you realize the mother is paying for the gown.

37. THE SITUATION: Two passengers riding in the backseat of a taxi give conflicting directions to the driver.

PASSENGERS: You are arguing with each other about the best way to get to your destination. You each insist that the driver follow your directions.

DRIVER: You already know the best way to get to the passengers' destination.

38. THE SITUATION: During rehearsal, a play director instructs an actor and actress to kiss each other at the end of a scene.

DIRECTOR: This kiss is very important to the play; you need them to perform it perfectly.

ACTRESS: You don't want to embarrass the actor by telling him, but he has terrible breath.

ACTOR: You want to please the director and perform the kiss well.

39. THE SITUATION: A realtor is showing a house to a married couple.

HUSBAND: You love this house and want to buy it.

WIFE: You hate this house and want to look at another.

REALTOR: You really want to sell this house today.

40. THE SITUATION: A trainer teaches two new supermarket cashiers how to operate a cash register.

FIRST CASHIER: You're a fast learner and want the trainer to go through the steps faster.

SECOND CASHIER: You're a slow learner and need the instructor to move through the steps slower.

TRAINER: You want to do your best to make sure both new cashiers are trained properly.

Love Is in the Air

Two Players

1. THE SITUATION: A man is enjoying a nice dinner with his girlfriend when she begins to ask about his past relationships.

> **WOMAN:** You think it's important for your boyfriend to be completely honest about his past.
>
> **MAN:** You want to keep your past in the past.

2. THE SITUATION: A woman speaks to her fiancé about the wedding gown she'd like to wear for their wedding.

> **WOMAN:** You don't want to wear a traditional white wedding gown. You want to wear something that includes a mix of bright and bold colors.
>
> **FIANCÉ:** You want your bride-to-be to dress in a conservative, traditional white wedding gown.

3. THE SITUATION: A girl speaks to a male friend about a plan she has to break up with her boyfriend.

> **GUY:** You are under the impression that this girl is in love with you, and you want to help her find a way to explain that to her current boyfriend.
>
> **GIRL:** You have no romantic interest in this guy; he's just a friend.

4. THE SITUATION: A guy confronts his girlfriend about her post on an online dating site advertising her availability.

> **GUY:** You're angry! You thought you had a great relationship with your girlfriend.
>
> **GIRLFRIEND:** Instead of explaining why you signed up for an online dating service, you want to know why your boyfriend is looking online for a date.

5. THE SITUATION: A girl asks her boyfriend to quit his job at the company where they both work because the company disapproves of co-workers dating each other.

> **GIRL:** You are afraid you might be fired if the company finds out your boyfriend is a co-worker. You think he should quit because you make more money than he does.
>
> **BOYFRIEND:** You think this policy is unfair, if not illegal.

6. THE SITUATION: A husband and wife are watching television. The wife begins to weep when a character on the show they're watching dies.

> **HUSBAND:** You're angry because your wife is crying about a fictional TV character but didn't show nearly as much emotion when your own mother died a few weeks ago.
>
> **WIFE:** You usually keep your emotions under control, but there was something about the death scene in this TV show that really moved you to tears.

7. THE SITUATION: A guy tells his girlfriend he'd like to move in with her.

> **GIRLFRIEND:** You're excited! You've been waiting for your boyfriend to ask you this for a long time.
>
> **GUY:** You want to move in only temporarily while your apartment is being painted.

8. THE SITUATION: A girl grabs her boyfriend's mobile phone and browses through his messages and photos.

> **GIRL:** You think your boyfriend is cheating on you, and you want to find a message or photo to prove it. However, you can't find anything incriminating.
>
> **BOYFRIEND:** You have nothing to hide and don't mind your girlfriend searching through your messages and photos.

9. THE SITUATION: A guy runs into his girlfriend at a mall. Earlier in the day, she told him she couldn't go on a movie date with him that night because she wasn't feeling well and needed to stay home and rest.

GUY: You're angry because your girlfriend clearly lied to you.

GIRL: You lied to your boyfriend because you didn't have the heart to tell him you'd rather go shopping than see a movie with him that night.

10. THE SITUATION: A girl tells her boyfriend she hates his new haircut and wants to "fix" it.

GIRL: You are certain you can repair your boyfriend's bad haircut with just a few snips.

BOYFRIEND: You don't think your girlfriend knows anything about cutting hair.

11. THE SITUATION: A girl sits silently beside her boyfriend, clearly annoyed with him about something.

GIRL: Your boyfriend obviously forgot that today is your birthday. You don't want to tell him outright why you're upset with him; you want him to figure it out on his own.

BOY: You can see that your girlfriend is angry with you about something, and you want to know what's wrong.

12. THE SITUATION: A husband asks his wife a question about his toothbrush.

HUSBAND: Lately you've noticed the bristles on your toothbrush seem to be wearing down quickly, and you're wondering if your wife has been using your toothbrush.

WIFE: Apparently, you've been using your husband's toothbrush to clean the rim under the toilet bowl. You thought it was an old, unused toothbrush!

13. THE SITUATION: A girl tells her boyfriend she wants to break up with him because he doesn't like chocolate.

GIRL: You recently discovered your boyfriend hates chocolate. You love chocolate and can't imagine having a boyfriend who does not share your love for it.

BOY: You think this is a ridiculous reason for breaking up with you. You're convinced there's another reason.

14. THE SITUATION: A girl speaks to her ex-boyfriend about an "I love you" text message she received from him yesterday.

GIRL: You were very upset when your ex-boyfriend broke up with you, but now you're thrilled because you think this message means he's changed his mind about breaking up.

BOY: You sent this message weeks ago … *before* you broke up with your girlfriend. You think the message must have been delayed somehow; you don't want to get back together with her.

15. THE SITUATION: A woman asks her husband why he repeated the name Shirley in his sleep last night.

WOMAN: You're convinced your husband is having an affair with someone named "Shirley," and you want him to confess.

MAN: When you were a child, you had a dog named Shirley. For some reason, you were dreaming about that dog last night.

16. THE SITUATION: A woman shows her engagement ring to her friend.

WOMAN: Your fiancé told you this ring had been in his family for years and it's worth tens of thousands of dollars. You're proud of both the ring and your fiancé, and you can't help but brag about him.

FRIEND: Only a few days ago, you saw the exact ring in a department store for a couple of hundred dollars.

17. THE SITUATION: A guy is upset with his girlfriend over the number of Xs (kisses) she included at the bottom of the last text message she sent him.

GIRL: You usually write five Xs at the bottom of your text messages to your boyfriend, but for some reason, you only included four in your last message to him. You think it's ridiculous for him to be so upset about it.

BOY: You notice there is one fewer X than usual in your girlfriend's text message to you, and you take it as a signal that she's preparing to break up with you.

18. **THE SITUATION:** A girl and her boyfriend are at a party playing charades. The girl acts out her phrase while the boyfriend is watching.

GIRL: Thinking it would be a creative way to deliver the news, you're miming the phrase "I am pregnant" to your boyfriend.

BOYFRIEND: You've been unhappy with your relationship for quite some time now, but you haven't had the guts to tell your girlfriend. You intend to break up with her after the party is over.

19. **THE SITUATION:** A girl and her new boyfriend discuss a party invitation they both received.

GIRL: You want to go to the party, but not with your boyfriend. Your ex-boyfriend is going to be at the party, and even though you don't intend to get back together with him, you don't want to create an awkward situation.

BOY: You want to go to the party, but not with your girlfriend. Your ex-girlfriend is going to be at the party, and even though you don't intend to get back together with her, you don't want to create an awkward situation.

20. **THE SITUATION:** A girl questions her boyfriend about his Facebook change in relationship status from "In a Relationship" to "Single."

GIRL: You're angry! You think your boyfriend is a coward for not telling you to your face that he wants to break up with you.

BOY: You never changed your relationship status. You suspect that your brother hacked into your account and changed it as a joke.

21. THE SITUATION: A guy and a girl who met on an online dating service meet for the first time.

GIRL: Your first impression of the guy is positive. You're expecting the date will be wonderful!

BOY: You didn't include in your online profile that you spent ten years in prison, but you feel that it's best to let the girl know now before anything further develops.

22. THE SITUATION: A brunette girl accuses her blonde friend of having a fling with her boyfriend because she found a blonde hair on his pillow.

BRUNETTE GIRL: You've always thought your friend had a thing for your boyfriend, and you're convinced the hair you found on your pillow is hers.

BLONDE GIRL: You haven't been fooling around with your friend's boyfriend. You think the hair she found is her own. Your friend recently changed her hair color from blonde to brunette!

23. THE SITUATION: A girl is concerned about the pained expression on her boyfriend's face as he proposes to her.

GIRL: You think your boyfriend is having second thoughts about marrying you and that's why he has a pained expression.

BOYFRIEND: You're in pain because you banged up your knee earlier that day. Still, you wanted to get down on one knee to propose, and doing so makes the pain worse.

24. THE SITUATION: A man accidentally refers to his wife Julia as "Amanda," the name of an ex-girlfriend.

HUSBAND: The second the name "Amanda" comes out of your mouth, you realize your error and desperately try to cover your mistake.

WIFE: You are angry and horrified when you hear your husband say his ex-girlfriend's name instead of yours.

25. THE SITUATION: A girl beats her boyfriend in an arm wrestling match.

GIRL: You've built up a great deal of muscle strength by lifting weights and exercising and wanted to show your boyfriend how strong you've become.

BOYFRIEND: You can't believe your girlfriend just beat you in arm wrestling.

26. THE SITUATION: A guy and his girlfriend often celebrate the anniversary of all their "firsts": first kiss, first movie date, first meal together, etc. Today, they are celebrating the anniversary of their first drink together.

GUY: You love to celebrate the anniversary of all your "firsts," and you're certain your girlfriend loves celebrating them, too.

GIRL: You're getting tired of all the celebrations. You went along with it for a while because your boyfriend seemed to love it so much, but now you think it's silly.

27. THE SITUATION: A girl decides to tell her best guy friend that his girlfriend has been cheating on him.

GIRL: You don't want to upset your best friend, but you feel he's better off knowing the truth about his girlfriend.

BEST FRIEND: You don't believe her. You think she wants you to split up with your girlfriend because she's in love with you and wants your girlfriend out of the picture.

28. THE SITUATION: A guy and a girl meet to discuss their feelings with each other.

GUY: You suspect this girl has feelings for you, but you are only interested in a friendship with her and nothing more.

GIRL: You suspect this guy has feelings for you, but you are only interested in a friendship with him and nothing more.

29. THE SITUATION: A girl had previously asked her friend to flirt with her boyfriend to test his fidelity. The boyfriend responded to her flirting, and the two discuss what happened.

GIRL: Instead of being angry with your boyfriend, you're angry with your girlfriend, accusing her of trying to steal your boyfriend from you.

FRIEND: You didn't want to participate in your girlfriend's scheme, but as a good friend, you decided to go through with it.

30. THE SITUATION: A guy tries to console his friend after hearing that his girlfriend broke up with him.

GUY: You feel bad for your friend and try to make him feel better by telling him he was too good for the girl.

FRIEND: You're feeling guilty because your girlfriend broke up with you after learning you'd been cheating on her.

Three Players

31. THE SITUATION: A husband and wife are grocery shopping when a woman approaches the husband and engages him in conversation.

HUSBAND: You've been cheating on your wife with this woman, who doesn't know you are married.

WIFE: You'd like to know how and why this strange woman knows your husband.

WOMAN: You've been seeing this man for the past few weeks but didn't know that he was married … until now.

32. THE SITUATION: A woman is enjoying a romantic dinner in a nice restaurant with a guy she's been dating for two weeks when a friend of the guy sees him and stops to say hello.

> **WOMAN:** You're an American woman who finds men with British accents sexy; that's what you find most attractive about this guy.
>
> **GUY:** You're not British. You're faking a British accent because you know this girl loves British men.
>
> **FRIEND:** You've known this guy for years. You know he's not British, and you're wondering why he's speaking with a British accent.

33. THE SITUATION: A guy and his ex-girlfriend speak to a mutual friend.

> **GUY:** You feel like the mutual friend was a better friend to your ex than to you, and you want him to remain your friend as well as your ex's. You don't want to lose him in the breakup.
>
> **GIRL:** You feel like the mutual friend was a better friend to your ex than to you, and you want him to remain your friend as well as your ex's. You don't want to lose him in the breakup.
>
> **MUTUAL FRIEND:** You intend to remain friends with both the girl and the guy.

34. THE SITUATION: A waiter in a restaurant takes a dinner order from a guy and his girlfriend and begins to flirt with the girl.

> **WAITER:** You find the girl very attractive and openly flirt with her, not caring that the girl is with her boyfriend.
>
> **GIRL:** You don't mind the flirting; in fact, you're enjoying it. You think it's harmless.
>
> **BOY:** The flirting bothers you, but instead of telling the waiter to stop, you pretend to be attracted to *him* and start flirting with him just to see how he responds.

35. THE SITUATION: A young man is on a blind date with a young woman he met online. To the young man's surprise, the woman brought her mom along with her!

> **WOMAN:** You need your mother's approval for everything you do in life, including the men you date. You don't intend for her to stay for the entire date; you just want her to meet him.

> **MAN:** You think it's bizarre that the woman brought her mom along, but since the woman is very attractive, you decide to stay and see what happens.

> **MOM:** You are attracted to this young man, and in spite of the fact that he is there to meet your daughter, you begin flirting with him.

36. THE SITUATION: Two girls talk about the many sweet things each of their boyfriends say to them and ask a third friend what kind of nice things her boyfriend says about her.

> **FIRST TWO FRIENDS:** Each of your boyfriends often tells you how pretty you are.

> **THIRD FRIEND:** Your boyfriend rarely says anything nice to you, and hearing what your two friends are saying makes you feel bad.

37. THE SITUATION: A guy and his girlfriend run into a mutual female friend. The friend is wearing a necklace that looks exactly like the one the guy gave his girlfriend for a birthday gift a few weeks ago.

> **GUY:** You think your girlfriend hated the birthday gift and gave it to her friend without telling you.

> **GIRLFRIEND:** You compliment the friend on her necklace and tell her that your generous boyfriend gave you one just like it for your birthday a few weeks ago.

> **FRIEND:** You bought the necklace for yourself a few days ago.

38. THE SITUATION: As a gift, a husband hires a professional chef to give his wife cooking lessons.

> **HUSBAND:** You think your wife is a great cook and would love to have a professional chef give her some tips to make her cooking even better.
>
> **WIFE:** You're insulted by this gift. You think this is your husband's way of telling you he hates your cooking.
>
> **CHEF:** You just want to do what you were hired to do as best you can.

39. THE SITUATION: A girl takes her boyfriend shopping for a new suit, and both ask the salesperson for her opinion on the one he's trying on.

> **GIRL:** Your boyfriend recently put on a few pounds, and you think the suit looks too tight on him.
>
> **BOYFRIEND:** You love the suit and think it looks great on you.
>
> **SALESPERSON:** You will say or do anything you have to in order to make this sale.

40. THE SITUATION: Two female friends stop a stranger on the street and ask him which of the two he'd be more inclined to date based on his first impression of them.

> **GIRLS:** Each of you is doing your best to get the guy to select you.
>
> **GUY:** You don't want to appear rude, but you aren't attracted to either one.

Family Matters

Two Players

1. THE SITUATION: A father speaks to his son about the dangers of alcohol just before the son is about to meet his friends for a drink at a local bar.

FATHER: You've always been a big drinker; you're actually a bit drunk right now. Even though you realize you're a hypocrite, you still think it's your duty to tell your son to be careful about drinking too much.

SON: You know your father is a big drinker, so it's difficult to take him seriously when he warns you about the dangers of drinking.

2. **THE SITUATION:** A mother shows her daughter a dress she bought for her to wear to her high school graduation party.

MOTHER: You love this dress, and you can't wait to see your daughter in it.

DAUGHTER: You love that your mother took the time to buy you a dress for your party, but you hate it.

3. **THE SITUATION:** A wife tells her husband that he takes too long to shower each morning.

WIFE: You're concerned about the water bill.

HUSBAND: You enjoy your time in the shower; you intend to keep taking long showers.

4. **THE SITUATION:** A girl tells her father that she intends to try out for the high school football team.

GIRL: You're a very athletic and competitive girl who loves football. You think you'd easily make the team, but you're not sure how your father would feel about it.

FATHER: You are thrilled that your daughter wants to play on the high school team, but you want to make sure she's aware of the challenges she will surely face from those who don't believe girls should be playing football.

5. **THE SITUATION:** A girl tells her brother that he needs to contribute more money to a gift for their parents' anniversary.

SISTER: Your brother always claims he has no money, yet he bought a new video game console for himself yesterday.

BROTHER: Your sister has a great job and makes a great deal of money. You think she can easily afford to put more money into your parents' gift.

6. THE SITUATION: The power goes out while a father and his daughter are watching television, and the father uses the opportunity to talk with his daughter.

> **FATHER:** You rarely talk to your daughter about what's happening in her life, and you think now is a great time to have a nice father-daughter chat with her.
>
> **DAUGHTER:** You rarely speak to your father, except when you need or want something from him. You're struggling to think of things about your life to discuss with him.

7. THE SITUATION: A husband tells his wife that their daughter was rude to his mother during her last visit.

> **HUSBAND:** You want your wife to speak to your daughter about the unkind things she said to your mother.
>
> **WIFE:** You don't like your husband's mother, and you don't blame your daughter for being rude to her.

8. THE SITUATION: A father shows his son a fancy new sports car he bought for himself.

> **FATHER:** You love this car; you can't wait to show it off to your neighbors and friends.
>
> **SON:** You think your father is too old to be driving a car like this.

9. THE SITUATION: A husband tells his wife that he just got off the phone with a representative from the IRS, who told him he owed the IRS thousands of dollars in unpaid taxes.

> **HUSBAND:** Fearing you would be arrested if you didn't immediately pay the IRS, you gave the representative on the phone your credit card information.
>
> **WIFE:** You are certain the call was a scam.

10. THE SITUATION: A teenage boy notices that his grandfather just bought a new smartphone for himself.

> **BOY:** You assume your grandfather doesn't know anything about how a smartphone works and want to teach him how to use it.
>
> **GRANDFATHER:** You know more about smartphones than your grandson thinks you do.

11. THE SITUATION: A boy offers his sister a free ticket to a film playing that night.

> **BOY:** Your parents are out of the house for the night, and you're planning to throw a party. You know your parents would not allow you to have an unsupervised party at your house. You also know your sister would tell them if you did.
>
> **GIRL:** Your brother's generosity makes you suspicious that he's up to something. It's unlike him to give you anything for free.

12. THE SITUATION: A sister tries to convince her brother that he needs to improve his grades and work harder in school.

> **GIRL:** You think your brother is intelligent and would do much better in school if he applied himself.
>
> **BOY:** You have no interest in school and are considering dropping out.

13. THE SITUATION: A mother questions her son about an "I hate you" text she received from him late last night.

> **MOTHER:** You suspect he sent you this text because you have yet to tell him you're planning to leave his father, whom your son loves dearly.
>
> **SON:** You were drinking heavily last night. You thought perhaps you sent a drunk text to your ex-girlfriend, but now you realize you accidentally sent it to your mother.

14. THE SITUATION: A boy is concerned about his father's weight gain.

BOY: Your father has been steadily putting on the pounds this past year, and you suggest that he start dieting and exercising.

FATHER: You think it's natural for people to gain weight with age; you're not concerned about your weight gain.

15. THE SITUATION: A mother speaks to her daughter about the daughter's obsession with losing weight.

DAUGHTER: You think you're overweight and need to lose at least ten pounds.

MOTHER: You believe your daughter's weight is ideal, and you're concerned about the way she perceives herself.

16. THE SITUATION: A mother speaks to her son about his weekend reading habits.

BOY: You love spending all of your free time reading.

MOTHER: You think it's strange that your son spends his weekends reading.

17. THE SITUATION: A father tells his son that he should be more like his older brother.

FATHER: Your older son is polite and respectful; you want your younger son to behave the same way.

SON: Your older brother only pretends to be nice to your father to get what he wants; you can't believe your father has been buying his act for as long as he has.

18. THE SITUATION: A boy tells his sister that she's eating a doughnut he previously licked.

BROTHER: You're angry because your sister is eating a doughnut you had asked her to save for you. You didn't really lick the doughnut.

SISTER: You feel sick at the thought of eating a doughnut your brother licked.

19. THE SITUATION: A father speaks to his daughter about the boy she is seeing.

> **DAUGHTER:** You tend to do whatever you like and don't care much about your father's opinion concerning boyfriends.
>
> **FATHER:** You actually like your daughter's boyfriend, but you think they should split up … because you feel your daughter isn't good enough for *him*!

20. THE SITUATION: A boy notices his mother did not participate in the standing ovation he received after singing a solo in his school's choir concert, and he wants to know why.

> **BOY:** You're upset because your mother did not stand along with everyone else in the audience.
>
> **MOTHER:** Although you love your son very much, you just don't think he is a very good singer. You believe it's important to be completely honest with him.

21. THE SITUATION: A girl compliments her father on how nice he looks.

> **GIRL:** You realize you don't often compliment your dad about anything, and you've decided that starting today you're going to be nicer to him.
>
> **FATHER:** Your daughter rarely has anything positive to say about you, so you think she's complimenting you because she wants something.

22. THE SITUATION: A mother offers his son's girlfriend one hundred dollars to break up with him.

> **MOTHER:** You can't stand this girl. You believe she doesn't really love your son and has been using him for all of the expensive gifts he gives her. You've shared your feelings about her with your son, but he refuses to believe you.
>
> **GIRLFRIEND:** You don't actually love your boyfriend, but you've stayed with him because he spends a lot of money on you.

23. THE SITUATION: A girl wants to know why her mother unfriended her on Facebook.

> **GIRL:** You can't believe your own mother unfriended you.
>
> **MOTHER:** Explain to your daughter that you unfriended her because you were tired of all her requests to play online games that don't interest you.

24. THE SITUATION: A boy tells his sister the goldfish she asked him to feed while she was away for the weekend died.

> **BROTHER:** You forgot about feeding the goldfish.
>
> **SISTER:** You're furious with your brother for forgetting to feed your goldfish.

25. THE SITUATION: A father watching a horror movie on television with his son wants to change the channel.

> **SON:** You're enjoying the movie and want to watch it to the end.
>
> **FATHER:** This movie is frightening you to death, and you want to switch the channel.

26. THE SITUATION: A boy presents his mother with a box of chocolates.

> **MOTHER:** Your son doesn't know that you are allergic to chocolate.
>
> **BOY:** Yesterday you made a casual remark that hurt your mother's feelings. The chocolate is a gift you're offering as part of an apology.

27. THE SITUATION: A father believes it's time to tell his young daughter that Santa Claus doesn't really exist.

> **FATHER:** You're struggling to find the right words to tell your daughter there is no Santa Claus.
>
> **DAUGHTER:** You've known there was no Santa Claus for years; you have pretended to believe to make your father happy.

28. THE SITUATION: The divorced mother of a teenage boy tells him that she's decided to remarry his father.

> **MOTHER:** You are happy to share this news with your son, whom you think will be thrilled.
>
> **SON:** You're not happy to hear this. You think your parents got along better with each other after they divorced.

29. THE SITUATION: A teenage girl notices her mother wearing a pair of jeans that the girl bought last week.

> **MOTHER:** You love to brag to your friends about how you can fit into your daughter's clothes.
>
> **DAUGHTER:** You hate it when your mother steals your clothes and think your outfits are much too tight on her.

30. THE SITUATION: A girl tries sneaking into her house late at night, when she runs into her younger sister. Their parents are asleep.

> **GIRL:** You think your sister may tell your parents that you broke curfew and want her to keep her mouth shut.
>
> **SISTER:** You know your parents will be angry to learn your sister broke curfew and realize you can use this information to your advantage.

Three Players

31. THE SITUATION: A mother and father talk to their daughter, a senior in high school, about her plans after graduation.

> **MOTHER:** You want your daughter to attend college and study medicine or law.
>
> **FATHER:** You want your daughter to follow her dreams and do something she loves after high school.
>
> **DAUGHTER:** You want to travel around the world after high school while you decide what you'd like to do with the rest of your life.

32. THE SITUATION: A son and a daughter ask their mother which of them is her favorite.

> **SON AND DAUGHTER:** You asked the question as a joke and assumed she would say that she has no favorite and loves you both the same.
>
> **MOTHER:** You know your kids are joking with you, but you turn the joke around and name one of them as your favorite, just to see their reaction.

33. THE SITUATION: A nervous mother and father decide to talk about "the birds and bees" with their teenage daughter.

> **MOTHER AND FATHER:** You're uncomfortable having this conversation and struggle to find the best way to talk about it.
>
> **DAUGHTER:** You know more about the facts of life than your parents realize, and you find their awkwardness amusing.

34. THE SITUATION: After a mother and father eat a dinner prepared by their daughter, the father proclaims it the best meal he's ever had.

> **DAUGHTER:** You're very happy that your father loves your cooking.
>
> **FATHER:** You didn't particularly like the meal, but you want to make your daughter happy, so you lie about how great it was.
>
> **MOTHER:** You're angry with your husband, thinking his praise for your daughter's cooking is his way of saying he doesn't like *your* cooking.

35. THE SITUATION: A mother and father present their daughter with a birthday cake.

> **MOTHER AND FATHER:** You are both happy to celebrate your daughter's birthday.
>
> **DAUGHTER:** Your birthday is next week. You can't believe your own parents don't remember the date of your birth.

36. THE SITUATION: A father meets his daughter's boyfriend for the first time.

> **FATHER:** Even though you are normally very protective of your daughter, your first impression of this young man is very positive.
>
> **BOYFRIEND:** You are a polite, respectful young man who treats your girlfriend very well.
>
> **GIRLFRIEND:** You know that your father doesn't normally approve of the boys you bring home … and you're hoping he doesn't approve of this one! You've recently met another boy you like better, but you don't have the courage to tell your current boyfriend. You are hoping to use your father's disapproval as an excuse for why you can't see him anymore.

37. THE SITUATION: A recently married woman meets her mother and her new mother-in-law for lunch.

> **MOTHER:** You're enjoying the company of your daughter's mother-in-law. In fact, you like her so much that you pay little attention to your own daughter and chat and laugh with the mother-in-law.
>
> **MOTHER-IN-LAW:** You're having a great time with your new in-law. You're so happy you have a new friend.
>
> **DAUGHTER:** You're a bit annoyed that your mother and mother-in-law are having such a good time together. It appears your mother is enjoying your mother-in-law's company more than yours!

38. THE SITUATION: For dessert, a mother offers her son an apple and her daughter a chocolate cookie.

> **SON:** You'd rather have the cookie.
>
> **DAUGHTER:** You'd rather have the apple.
>
> **MOTHER:** You think your son needs to lose weight and your daughter needs to gain weight.

39. THE SITUATION: A husband and his pregnant wife speak to their obstetrician about the gender of their unborn baby.

> **HUSBAND:** You want to know the gender of the baby.
>
> **WIFE:** You want the gender of the baby to be a surprise.
>
> **OBSTETRICIAN:** You are stuck in the middle and suggest that the couple needs to decide between themselves whether or not they want him to reveal the gender.

40. THE SITUATION: Two sisters ask their mother for her opinion on which of them is better dressed for a party they're about to attend.

> **SISTERS:** You each believe you are more fashionable than the other.
>
> **MOTHER:** You don't like how either daughter is dressed and think they both should change into something else.

Out and About

Two Players

1. THE SITUATION: Two friends meet in a bar during happy hour.

> **FIRST FRIEND:** Your friend retired from his job about a year ago and has since put on quite a few pounds. You are concerned about your friend's health, and you think his weight gain is due to his lack of activity and extravagant lifestyle.
>
> **SECOND FRIEND:** You retired from your job about a year ago, and since then, you've been having the time of your life, eating out all the time, and partying every weekend. You don't intend to slow down anytime soon.

2. THE SITUATION: A guy offers his friend a ride on his new motorcycle.

> **GUY:** You're excited about your new motorcycle, and you want to share your excitement with your friend.

FRIEND: You're deathly afraid of motorcycles, but you don't want your friend to know that. Still, the last thing you want to do is ride on a motorcycle.

3. THE SITUATION: A woman approaches a stranger in the lobby of a movie theater to tell her to stop staring at her husband.

> **WOMAN:** You've seen this woman giving your husband the eye while you were waiting in line to buy tickets.
>
> **STRANGER:** You have no idea what this crazy woman is talking about. You weren't looking at her husband.

4. THE SITUATION: A guy asks his friend to return his mobile phone.

> **GUY:** You want your phone back; you need to make a call.
>
> **FRIEND:** You had taken your friend's phone into the bathroom and accidentally dropped it into the toilet. Now it doesn't work.

5. THE SITUATION: A young woman offers an older man her seat on a crowded bus.

> **YOUNG WOMAN:** You are a considerate person, and you insist that the man takes your seat.
>
> **OLDER MAN:** You wouldn't dream of taking the woman's seat. You are in fine health and perfectly capable of standing.

6. THE SITUATION: Two strangers study a painting in a modern-art museum.

> **FIRST PERSON:** You think the painting is awful and share your opinion with the stranger standing beside you.
>
> **SECOND PERSON:** You are the artist of this painting, and you're extremely proud of your work.

7. THE SITUATION: Two friends discuss their gym membership.

> **FIRST FRIEND:** You used to see your friend in the gym every day, but you haven't seen her there in quite a while. You are a strong proponent of exercise and healthy living.

SECOND FRIEND: You haven't been to the gym in weeks. You've become tired of counting calories and working hard to keep in shape. You've decided to embrace the philosophy that all people should be happy with their size and weight, no matter what they look like.

8. THE SITUATION: Two friends are having breakfast together in a diner.

FIRST FRIEND: You're focused on your phone, texting other friends and ignoring your friend in the diner.

SECOND FRIEND: You're annoyed by your friend's rudeness.

9. THE SITUATION: A guy tells his drunk friend that what's happening right now is actually a dream.

MAN: Your friend is very drunk, and you love playing pranks on him.

FRIEND: Since you believe you are in a dream, you try to fly but become frustrated when you are unable to lift off the ground after flapping your arms wildly.

10. THE SITUATION: A man pulls a woman out of the way of an oncoming car, saving her life.

MAN: You risked your own life to save this woman.

WOMAN: Instead of thanking this man for saving your life, you're angry because his pull caused you to break one of your heels.

11. THE SITUATION: Two friends show up at a party wearing the same dress.

FIRST FRIEND: You're embarrassed to be wearing the same dress as your friend.

SECOND FRIEND: You find it funny to be wearing the same dress as your friend and want to sit or stand beside her all night and laugh about it.

12. **THE SITUATION:** Two strangers sit beside each other in a movie theater, watching a film.

> **FIRST PERSON:** You are having trouble understanding the film and continually ask the guy sitting beside you questions about the characters and plot.
>
> **SECOND PERSON:** You're trying to focus on the film, but the guy sitting beside you keeps asking you questions about it.

13. **THE SITUATION:** Two female friends who haven't seen each other in years run into each other in a park.

> **FIRST FRIEND:** You've put on a bit of weight since you've last seen your friend.
>
> **SECOND FRIEND:** It appears that your old friend is pregnant, and you'd like to congratulate her.

14. **THE SITUATION:** A man stops a woman on the street and asks if she wouldn't mind if he took a picture of her.

> **MAN:** This woman looks exactly like your dearly departed wife, and even though you know the woman is a stranger, you'd love to have a photo of her to show your friends.
>
> **WOMAN:** You find this man very strange, and you don't like the idea of having your photo taken by him. Still, you're interested in knowing why he wants to take your picture.

15. **THE SITUATION:** Two friends are engaged in conversation, when one of them says he thinks he's having a heart attack.

> **FIRST FRIEND:** You know your friend likes to play pranks on you, and you think he's pretending to have a heart attack for a laugh.
>
> **SECOND FRIEND:** You're in intense pain and need medical attention immediately!

16. **THE SITUATION:** A police officer approaches a man who appears to be breaking into a car. The man insists the car is his and his keys and identification are locked inside.

MAN: The car doesn't belong to you. You are breaking into this car for the purpose of stealing it.

POLICE OFFICER: You don't know whether or not to believe this man. You can't run the license plate because your police scanner is broken.

17. THE SITUATION: A woman cries after a beggar asks her for money.

WOMAN: You're crying because you lost your job today. You are deep in debt and have no money to offer this beggar.

BEGGAR: You hate seeing this woman cry, and you want to do what you can to comfort her. You don't have much money on you, but you offer her some.

18. THE SITUATION: A man at a party notices an attractive woman glancing at him and giggling.

MAN: You think this woman is giggling because she's attracted to you.

WOMAN: You're giggling at this man because he has a huge zit on the tip of his nose.

19. THE SITUATION: A guy in a gym brags to a girl about the number of pushups he can do.

GUY: You think this girl is cute, and you're trying to impress her. The truth is that you couldn't do more than ten pushups if your life depended on it.

GIRL: You'd love to see how many pushups this guy can do.

20. THE SITUATION: A man complains to his neighbor about the dog poop he finds on his lawn every morning.

MAN: You believe your neighbor walks his dog late each night and allows it to poop on your lawn.

NEIGHBOR: You don't own a dog.

21. THE SITUATION: A girl meets her friend to tell her she just got engaged.

GIRL: You're very excited about your engagement, and you can't wait to share the news with your friend.

FRIEND: You love your friend, and you want what's best for her. You've known your friend's fiancé for quite a while, but you've never approved of him. You didn't think the relationship would last, so you never let her know your real feelings. Now you feel you must tell her.

22. THE SITUATION: It's Halloween. A man in his mid-thirties who is holding an open bag but not dressed in any type of costume, rings the doorbell of a neighborhood home and shouts, "Trick or Treat!" when the door opens.

> **MAN AT THE DOOR:** You think this man is too old to be trick-or-treating, and you also believe a costume is required for all trick-or-treaters. You refuse to give the man any candy and inquire about his age and lack of costume.

> **TRICK-OR-TREATER:** You want the man to believe that you *are* wearing a costume and tell him you are actually a young teenage girl made up to look like an older man.

23. THE SITUATION: A guy brags to his friend about how great he is at bowling.

> **GUY:** Every time you've bowled with your friend, you've won.

> **FRIEND:** You're tired of listening to your bragging friend. Truthfully, you always let him win because he's such a sore loser.

24. THE SITUATION: Two people are stuck in an elevator between floors, when one of them begins to remove the button panel.

> **FIRST PERSON:** You think some wires must be crossed inside the button panel and that's why the elevator stopped. You're removing the panel to see if you can find a problem.

> **SECOND PERSON:** You can't believe this guy is removing the panel. You're sure he will make the situation worse.

25. THE SITUATION: A girl tells her friend that she had to have her dog put down last night.

> **GIRL:** You don't appear to be sad or upset. You loved your dog, but you are actually relieved that the dog was put down because he was in pain for a long time. You're glad he's no longer suffering.
>
> **FRIEND:** You don't understand why your friend doesn't appear to be upset; you want her to let her feelings out.

26. THE SITUATION: A man wakes up on a sofa in a strange apartment and sees a woman looking at him.

> **MAN:** You know you were drinking heavily at a bar last night, but you don't know how you got to this apartment or who this woman is.
>
> **WOMAN:** You saw this drunken man stumbling along a road last night and kindly took him to your apartment to let him sleep it off on your sofa.

27. THE SITUATION: A female wedding guest asks a male guest why he is standing among a group of women just before the bride is about to toss her bouquet to them.

> **FEMALE GUEST:** You maintain that the bouquet toss is for women only; you want the guy to sit down.
>
> **MALE GUEST:** You don't see why you shouldn't be included among the women. You're single, and you think catching a bouquet will bring you the luck you need to find a mate.

28. THE SITUATION: A casually dressed husband and wife walk into a party and, to their surprise, see the male guests dressed in tuxedos and the women wearing formal gowns.

> **WIFE:** Even though you're underdressed, you don't want to leave because this looks like a great party!
>
> **HUSBAND:** You're embarrassed, and you want to leave!

29. THE SITUATION: A guy at a party is enjoying some snacks, but his friend tells him that he's eating dog treats.

GUY: You thought you were eating some kind of tasty party snack, and you're disgusted when you find out that they're dog treats.

FRIEND: You're pulling a prank on your friend; he's not eating dog treats.

30. THE SITUATION: A police officer gets out of his cruiser and gives a ticket to a man for driving with a broken headlight, but the driver notices the police cruiser also has a broken headlight.

MAN: You don't think it's fair for the officer to write you a ticket for an infraction he committed himself.

OFFICER: You thank the driver for letting you know about the headlight, but give him the ticket anyway.

Three Players

31. THE SITUATION: Two female friends are both interested in a man they see at a party and simultaneously approach him.

FIRST WOMAN: You are annoyed with your friend for showing interest in this man because you are single and she already has a boyfriend.

SECOND WOMAN: Although you already have a boyfriend, you enjoy flirting with single men.

MAN: You are not interested in either one of these women, but you don't want to appear rude to either one.

32. THE SITUATION: Three friends are in a karaoke bar. One of the friends is drunk and wants to sing a song.

DRUNKEN FRIEND: In your drunkenness, you believe you are an amazing singer.

FIRST FRIEND: You're afraid your drunken friend will embarrass himself.

SECOND FRIEND: You think your drunken friend's performance will be hysterical and would love to hear him sing.

33. THE SITUATION: Three friends are at a concert in a large outdoor venue. One announces he has to use the bathroom, but the lines in front of the restrooms are incredibly long. He's considering relieving himself behind some cars in the parking lot.

> **FIRST FRIEND:** You have to urinate badly. You'd rather use a bathroom, but you're not sure how long you can "hold it in."
>
> **SECOND FRIEND:** You think urinating in public is disgusting, not to mention illegal.
>
> **THIRD FRIEND:** You don't have a problem with urinating behind a car; you've done it many times yourself.

34. THE SITUATION: A bartender asks to see the ID of one of two women sitting together at his bar.

> **BARTENDER:** One of the women definitely looks older than twenty-one, but you're not so sure about the other. You only want to check the ID of the woman in question.
>
> **FIRST WOMAN:** You're older than twenty-one, but bartenders often check your ID. You don't mind; you're actually flattered when they do.
>
> **SECOND WOMAN:** You think you look younger than your friend, and you feel insulted when the bartender checks her ID but not yours.

35. THE SITUATION: A guy informs his two friends that a mutual friend passed away yesterday.

> **GUY:** You're sad to share this news with your two friends, whom you believe will both be very upset by the news.
>
> **FIRST FRIEND:** You are overcome with grief; you were very close with the deceased.
>
> **SECOND FRIEND:** You're upset but not because your friend died: The deceased owed you a great sum of money, and now you know you won't get it back.

36. THE SITUATION: Two guys are watching a football game on television at their friend's house and find out he has no beer to offer them.

HOST: You thought it would be nice to serve champagne instead of beer to your friends during the game.

FIRST GUY: You strongly believe that football and beer go together and offer to run out and get some.

SECOND GUY: You'd rather drink beer while watching the game, but you politely drink the champagne instead.

37. **THE SITUATION:** A guy asks his two friends if they'd consider adding him to their bowling team.

GUY: You think you're a pretty good bowler and you'd make an excellent addition to your friends' team.

FIRST FRIEND: You know your friend is not a great bowler, but you'd still welcome him to your team. To you, your friendship is more important than having a successful team.

SECOND FRIEND: You know your friend is not a great bowler, and you don't want him on the team. Still, you don't want to hurt his feelings.

38. **THE SITUATION:** A girl attempts to teach her two friends how to dance with each other.

GIRL: You're a good dancer who's also very impatient.

TWO FRIENDS: You're both not very coordinated when it comes to dancing, but you desperately want to learn how to dance with each other.

39. **THE SITUATION:** A girl asks two friends for their help in playing a practical joke on a mutual friend.

GIRL: You have a great idea for a practical joke to play on your friend, but you need the help of these two friends to pull it off.

FIRST FRIEND: You love practical jokes, and you're anxious to help.

SECOND FRIEND: You hate practical jokes, believing they often have a negative effect on friendships.

40. THE SITUATION: A guy asks his two friends for their opinion of a love poem he's written and plans to send to his girlfriend.

GUY: This is your first attempt at writing poetry, and you're not sure if your girlfriend will like it.

FIRST FRIEND: You love the poem and think his girlfriend will love it.

SECOND FRIEND: You think that the poem is juvenile and his girlfriend will think it's awful.

USING CONTRASTS

Neil Simon discovered that if you take a character who is hopelessly sloppy and have him live with a neatness fanatic, the possibilities for a play are almost endless. In fact, enough situations resulted from this combination of character types to keep *The Odd Couple* television series going for several years. Think of some popular plays, films, and television shows. How many of them involve leading characters that have diametrically opposed personalities?

The improvisation starters in this chapter provide contrasting character traits or emotions. The instructor or moderator should simply have the players take the stage, assign each one an indicated trait or emotion, and then read aloud the scene summary. Remind your players of the same rules described in chapter one, with the addition of the following: Everything you do and say should be consistent with your character's personality or emotional state, but avoid stereotypes. There is more than one way to express shyness, anxiety, frustration, elation, etc. Each person is unique; don't use clichéd means of expressing your character.

In some cases, the trait or emotion one should assign each player will be obvious. But in others, the trait or emotion can be randomly assigned. It might be fun to run some of these improvisations twice, having the players switch their traits the second time. For example, when presenting the first situation about a dance instructor teaching a new student a few basic dance steps, it would seem more sensible to characterize the dance instructor as enthusiastic and the new student as introverted, but running the improvisation a second time with an introverted instructor and an enthusiastic student would certainly create an entirely different scene.

You may use the following guide questions when discussing the performances with your players and audience:

- What specific conflicts resulted from the contrasting character traits or emotions portrayed by the players?
- Did the players *talk* about their characteristics, or did they *show* they possessed them? Did you notice any specific vocal or visible adjustments that were made to communicate their characteristics?
- Did the players' traits or emotions seem honest and natural, or were they contrived?
- Did the improvisation develop as you expected, or were you surprised by the direction in which it turned?

As in chapter one, most of the situations do not require gender-specific characters. Feel free to switch male references to female and female references to male.

Note: It might be a good idea to have a dictionary handy while running these improvisations. Dictionary definitions of the words assigned to the players may provide nuances that could help the players develop more specific objectives and motivations.

Two Players

1. ENTHUSIASTIC/INTROVERTED
A dance instructor teaches a new student a few basic dance steps.

2. ACTIVE/INACTIVE
A runner encourages a friend to go for a run with him.

3. OPTIMISTIC/PESSIMISTIC
Two friends buy lottery tickets at a convenience store.

4. IMPASSIONED/BEWILDERED
A psychic reader warns a client about a danger lurking in his future.

5. COMPASSIONATE/UNSYMPATHETIC

A teacher and her assistant discuss the best strategy for dealing with a problem child.

6. UNPATRIOTIC/PATRIOTIC

Two young men discuss the idea of joining the military.

7. REMORSEFUL/UNFORGIVING

A girl apologizes to her friend for telling lies about her.

8. REFINED/CRUDE

Two girls share dating stories with each other.

9. DECEPTIVE/FORTHRIGHT

While dusting a shelf, two cleaning women accidentally break an expensive crystal vase and discuss how to explain to the homeowner what happened.

10. SARDONIC/NAÏVE

A girl compliments her friend's singing.

11. SOMBER/FLIPPANT

A doctor warns his patient about the health risks of his smoking habit.

12. OUTSPOKEN/TACTFUL

Two teachers chat about the competence of their school's administrative staff.

13. SKILLFUL/INCOMPETENT

An auto mechanic trains a new employee.

14. GENEROUS/STINGY

Two restaurant patrons discuss the tip amount they should leave.

15. STRICT/LENIENT

A high school principal and his assistant modify their school's disciplinary code.

16. TASTELESS/TASTEFUL

A husband and wife shop for furniture for their new house.

17. RESOURCEFUL/INEPT

After locking themselves out of their house, a brother and sister try to get back inside.

18. EMPATHETIC/UNFEELING

Two girls in a movie theater watch a heart-wrenching scene from a sad movie.

19. ARDENT/CYNICAL

A research scientist tells a colleague that he has discovered a cure for the common cold.

20. ENVIOUS/CONTENT

Two girls at a party notice another girl across the room kissing an extremely attractive guy.

21. ORGANIZED/DISORGANIZED

Two roommates arrange books on a large bookcase.

22. DISCRIMINATING/UNDEMANDING

Two friends sample different wines at a wine tasting party.

23. INCONSIDERATE/NETTLED

Coughing and sneezing, a man enters a doctor's waiting room and sits beside someone reading a magazine.

24. JITTERY/COMPOSED

A police officer attempts to defuse a time bomb strapped to a man's waist.

25. VIVACIOUS/DISHEARTENED

A wrestler congratulates his opponent after winning the match.

26. SECURE/INSECURE

Two middle-aged women consider the reasons they're both single.

27. INEXPLICIT/CONFUSED

During rehearsal, a play director tells an actor that he's over-acting.

28. EMOTIONAL/UNEMOTIONAL

Two hospital nurses review a dying patient's chart.

29. BIG-THINKING/SMALL-THINKING

Two sisters plan a fiftieth birthday party for their father.

30. LAGGARD/ENERGETIC

Two guys in a gym prepare to work out.

31. HOPEFUL/HOPELESS

A man wearing a sign that reads, "The World Will End Tomorrow" speaks to a passerby.

32. AIMLESS/METHODICAL

Two sisters fold laundry for their mother.

33. IMITATIVE/ORIGINAL

Two singers/songwriters compose songs for their nightclub act.

34. OPTIMISTIC/FATALISTIC

A doctor informs a patient that his blood pressure is running a bit high.

35. VINDICTIVE/FORGIVING

Two girls discuss how to deal with a former friend who has spread vicious rumors about them.

36. EGOCENTRIC/UNASSUMING

Two students debate the difficulty of an exam they just completed.

37. CRITICAL/PRAISING

During intermission, two theatergoers critique the first act of a play.

38. EVASIVE/DIRECT

A tenant informs his landlord that he's not able to make a rent payment this month.

39. SELF-ASSURED/DOUBTFUL

Two actors talk about how they fared during a recent audition.

40. INSISTENT/OBSTINATE

A bartender encourages one of his regulars to try a new brand of beer instead of what he usually orders.

41. CALM/NERVOUS

Two patients in an office wait to see the dentist.

42. LOYAL/DISLOYAL

After years of using the same hair stylist, two girls discuss whether or not they should try someone new.

43. EXTRAVAGANT/MODERATE

Two roommates prepare to decorate their apartment for the winter holidays.

44. APPRECIATIVE/UNGRATEFUL

Two furniture deliverymen accept a tip from a customer.

45. DUBIOUS/CONFIDENT

Two high school seniors discuss their chances of receiving college acceptance letters.

46. INQUISITIVE/ENIGMATIC

A mental health counselor analyzes a patient.

47. ARTICULATE/INARTICULATE

A recruiter for an employment agency asks a client about his work experience.

48. GULLIBLE/SUSPICIOUS

A husband tells his wife that he just received a letter saying he won a trip to the Bahamas.

49. INHIBITED/UNINHIBITED

Two girls mingle at a party filled with people they don't know well.

50. FRUGAL/EXTRAVAGANT

A brother and sister discuss how much money to spend on a holiday gift for their parents.

51. CAUTIOUS/FEARLESS

Two doctors in an operating room try a new surgical technique on a heart patient.

52. COWARDLY/BRAVE

Two guys hear screams coming from inside a dark house.

53. MODEST/IMMODEST

Two girls shop for swimsuits.

54. FRIENDLY/UNFRIENDLY

A receptionist in a doctor's office greets a new patient.

55. PERCEPTIVE/UNOBSERVANT

Two guys at a magic show analyze the magician's act.

56. CREATIVE/UNIMAGINATIVE

Two gardeners arrange shrubs and flowers in a garden.

57. PROUD/HUMBLE

Two high school students accept a Certificate of Academic Excellence from their principal.

58. HARDWORKING/LAZY

A worker asks a co-worker to help him move a pile of bricks from one area of a construction site to another.

59. DISORIENTED/ORIENTED

Two travelers reach a fork in the road and discuss which direction to take.

60. ENGAGING/SHY

A masseuse prepares to massage a new client.

61. APATHETIC/CARING

A shopper in a supermarket tells the manager there's a little boy in the store who's crying because he can't find his mother.

62. ROMANTIC/UNROMANTIC

Two girls in a store shop for Valentine's Day cards for their boyfriends.

63. UNMINDFUL/CONSIDERATE

Two students walk into a classroom ten minutes late for their class.

64. CULTURED/UNREFINED

Two friends eat dinner in an elegant restaurant.

65. POSITIVE/DIFFIDENT

Two nominees for Employee of the Month in an advertising firm discuss their chances of winning.

66. IMPRESSIONABLE/SKEPTICAL

A skin care specialist advises a client to try a new conditioner to improve her skin's appearance.

67. IMPULSIVE/DELIBERATE

Two people shop for guitars in a music store.

68. TOLERANT/DEMANDING

An architect presents a client with plans for a new home.

69. ADAPTABLE/INFLEXIBLE

Two friends consider changing their usual plans for the weekend.

70. RATIONAL/UNREASONABLE

A dietitian offers a healthy meal plan to a prospective client.

71. INTELLIGENT/STUPID

Two shoppers in a bookstore search for weekend reading material.

72. TENACIOUS/IRRESOLUTE

A big-league baseball scout tries to recruit a talented college player.

73. COMPLEX/SIMPLE

Two dieters discuss the best way to lose five pounds.

74. DOMINEERING/SUBMISSIVE

A boy tries to persuade his younger brother to do his chores for him.

75. FOCUSED/DISTRACTED

Two burglars pry the lock of a door in an attempt to break into a house.

76. PERSISTENT/IRRESOLUTE

An IRS agent audits a businessman suspected of falsifying his federal tax return.

77. STUDIOUS/NEGLIGENT

Two students compare their individual methods of test preparation.

78. CALCULATING/ARTLESS

A student explains to her teacher why she couldn't complete her homework assignment.

79. FORMAL/INFORMAL

A husband and wife disagree about where to make a dinner reservation for their tenth wedding anniversary celebration.

80. ANXIOUS/UNWORRIED

Two friends discuss the idea of quitting their jobs and going into business together.

81. REALISTIC/IMPRACTICAL

An employee in a flower shop asks her manager for a 10-percent raise.

82. PATIENT/IMPATIENT

Two commuters wait for a train that was scheduled to arrive ten minutes earlier.

83. DISTRESSED/SANGUINE

A new hair stylist, fresh out of beauty school, meets her first client.

84. CONVENTIONAL/UNCONVENTIONAL

Two office workers exchange thoughts on their company's decision to eliminate casual Fridays.

85. SHREWD/NAÏVE

A salesman tries to sell a used car to a potential buyer.

86. LOQUACIOUS/QUIET

Two old friends who haven't seen each other in years run into each other.

87. ASSERTIVE/UNSURE

A high school student tries to convince his friend to skip school with him.

88. CLEVER/SIMPLE

Two guys attempt to crash a party.

89. GLOOMY/CHEERFUL

Two girls discuss how to spend a rainy afternoon.

90. NOSY/UNCONCERNED

Two girls at a party watch a boy across the room whisper into a girl's ear.

91. EMPATHETIC/UNFEELING

Two jurors deliberate the defendant's guilt in a murder trial.

92. CHUMMY/UNSOCIABLE

A woman orders a cup of coffee from a barista.

93. CONSTANT/CAPRICIOUS

Two girls discuss the pros and cons of having only one boyfriend instead of several at the same time.

94. IRRITATED/PERPLEXED

A man tells his optometrist that his new prescription eyeglasses made his vision worse.

95. SUPERFICIAL/GENUINE

Two men share their opinions on the characteristics of an ideal woman.

96. STRAIGHTFORWARD/CONTRADICTORY

A substance abuse counselor warns a young man about the dangers of drug abuse.

97. SPONTANEOUS/RIGID

Two vacationers plan a day at a beach resort.

98. DEVIOUS/TRUSTING

An office clerk tells his boss that he needs to leave work because he doesn't feel well.

99. PASSIONATE/CALM

Two football fans watch the last few seconds of a close game.

100. HONEST/DISHONEST

Two restaurant diners notice they were undercharged for an item on their bill.

101. CONCILIATORY/ANTAGONISTIC

Two basketball coaches compare strategies for improving their team's performance.

102. EMBARRASSED/COMPOSED

A girl helps her boyfriend stand after he trips over his own feet and falls on his face.

103. STERN/YIELDING

A mother and father try to decide on a weekend curfew time for their teenage daughter.

104. INDULGING/ABSTAINING

Two guys view the choices at an all-you-can-eat buffet.

105. ADVENTUROUS/FEARFUL

A hairstylist suggests a new design to a regular client.

106. CANTANKEROUS/GOOD-NATURED

Two shoppers shop for gifts in a crowded shopping mall during the holiday season.

107. STRAIGHTFORWARD/COMPLICATED

Two girls devise a plan to get their friend to a surprise party.

108. FEARLESS/APPREHENSIVE

Two boys in an amusement park consider taking a ride on an enormous roller coaster.

109. HEADSTRONG/CAUTIOUS

A public relations specialist offers ideas to a professional football player to advance the player's reputation.

110. DECEITFUL/INGENUOUS

A guy tells his girlfriend that the rumors she heard about him cheating on her are untrue.

111. BOISTEROUS/SOLEMN

A brother and sister attend their uncle's wake.

112. DISCIPLINED/UNDISCIPLINED

Two guys on a low-calorie diet discuss what to order for lunch.

113. MATURE/IMMATURE

Two high school students are eating lunch in the cafeteria when a food fight breaks out.

114. COMPOSED/OBNOXIOUS

A customer service representative in a department store explains to a customer why the bed sheets she bought last month are not returnable.

115. ELEGANT/PLAIN

Two chefs revise their restaurant's menu.

116. INTENSE/LOW-KEY

Two teens play each other in a video game.

117. AGITATED/REASSURING

A homeowner hires an exterminator to treat his home for an infestation of cockroaches.

118. AGGRESSIVE/APOLOGETIC

Two strangers accidentally bump into each other on a crowded street.

119. COURTEOUS/ANNOYED

A restaurant hostess informs a diner that there is an hour wait for a table.

120. CONFORMIST/NONCONFORMIST

A woman gives her friend wardrobe suggestions for an upcoming job interview.

121. METICULOUS/IMPRECISE

Two accountants prepare tax reports for their respective clients.

122. EMOTIONAL/DISPASSIONATE

Two baseball players walk off the field together after losing the final game of a championship series.

123. DISCONTENTED/CONTENTED

A girl and her boyfriend discuss the future of their relationship.

124. SELF-EFFACING/PRETENTIOUS

After their season has ended, two football players reflect on their individual accomplishments.

125. TRADITIONAL/AVANT-GARDE

Two sculptors discuss ideas for a statue they've been commissioned to design together.

126. UNSCRUPULOUS/SUSPICIOUS

A plumber hands a customer a bill that includes charges for work not specified on the estimate.

127. MODERN/OLD-FASHIONED

Two friends try on dresses in a boutique.

128. SENSIBLE/UNREASONABLE

An insurance agent recommends that her client buy additional life insurance.

129. DARING/CAUTIOUS

Two swimmers consider diving off a high cliff into a river below.

130. EAGER/UNEXCITED

A husband and wife receive a dinner invitation from the wife's mother.

131. PRACTICAL/EXTRAVAGANT

A financial advisor recommends that his client cut back on spending.

132. DECISIVE/INDECISIVE

A couple in a restaurant discusses menu options before ordering.

133. REGRETFUL/CONTENT

Two old men reflect on some of their life decisions and accomplishments.

134. IMAGINATIVE/STOLID

A manicurist in a salon suggests new designs to a client.

135. LOGICAL/IRRATIONAL

A father speaks to his child about the importance of behaving properly in a restaurant.

136. PRACTICAL/UNREALISTIC

A banker explains loan options to a customer.

137. CLUMSY/GRACEFUL

Two friends take tennis lessons.

138. RELAXED/TENSE

Two people in a car are stuck in a traffic jam.

139. SUAVE/UNREFINED

Two guys compare strategies for picking up girls in a museum.

140. BLUNT/TACTFUL

A couple responds to their friend's request to be godparents for her child.

141. GARRULOUS/QUIET

A bartender serves a drink to a lone customer sitting at his bar.

142. PREDICTABLE/ORIGINAL

Two kids choose different-colored crayons for pictures of puppies in their coloring books.

143. ABRASIVE/SOOTHING

A husband and wife try to quiet their crying baby.

144. DERISIVE/RESPECTFUL

Two students comment on their teacher's new haircut.

145. PRIVATE/OPEN

Two girls share details with each other about their first dates with their boyfriends.

146. METICULOUS/IMPRECISE

Two construction workers measure and cut lumber for a house they're building.

147. CONSCIENTIOUS/WASTEFUL

A girl asks her mother to switch from plastic bags to reusable shopping bags for grocery shopping.

148. OBVIOUS/INCONSPICUOUS

Two thieves steal wristwatches from a countertop in a jewelry store.

149. VERSATILE/LIMITED

Two singers preparing for an upcoming concert compare their song selections.

150. CIRCUMSPECT/UNGUARDED

A politician and his chief advisor develop strategies for an upcoming debate.

Three Players

151. ARDENT/KINDHEARTED/UNCHARITABLE

A man solicits two strangers for contributions to a worthy cause.

152. DOWNCAST/COMPASSIONATE/UNSYMPATHETIC

A guy tells two friends about his bad day.

153. DISTRESSED/HELPFUL/INEPT

A stranded motorist asks two strangers for assistance.

154. OPINIONATED/OPEN-MINDED/NARROW-MINDED

Three political analysts share their opinion on which U.S. President was the greatest.

155. COMPETITIVE/INCONSISTENT/CONSISTENT

A baseball coach explains to two of his pitchers why he chose one over the other to start in next week's game.

156. PLEASANT/AGREEABLE/DISAGREEABLE

Three college roommates consider ideas for decorating their dorm room.

157. INSECURE/ENCOURAGING/INSULTING

An artist shows his painting to two art critics.

158. STRAIGHTFORWARD/DEFENSIVE/REPENTANT

A sales manager in a department store criticizes two employees for their poor sales performance.

159. INDECISIVE/DISCOURAGING/ENCOURAGING

A girl tells her two friends that she's considering running a marathon.

160. COMPROMISING/ARGUMENTATIVE/AGREEABLE

A marriage therapist counsels a husband and wife.

161. ENCOURAGING/INDEPENDENT/DEPENDENT

A father tells his two grown children that he thinks it's time they leave home and find a place of their own.

162. INVESTIGATIVE/INCISIVE/RAMBLING

A police detective asks two burglary suspects to account for their whereabouts on the night of a recent home break-in.

163. AGGRESSIVE/INEFFECTIVE/UNCOOPERATIVE

Two federal agents interrogate a murder suspect.

164. STARSTRUCK/CHARISMATIC/INELEGANT

A girl asks two famous actors for their autographs.

165. EXHILARATED/DYNAMIC/RESERVED

A teenage girl tells her two friends that she was just accepted into the college of her choice.

166. STRICT/RESPECTFUL/DEFIANT

A mother commands her two children to clean their rooms.

167. DESPERATE/COURAGEOUS/COWARDLY

A woman whose cat is trapped in a burning house seeks the help of two strangers.

168. HESITANT/CRASS/DELICATE

A guy asks his two friends for advice about how to ask out a girl that interests him.

169. EXTRAVAGANT/FRUGAL/SWANKY

A wedding planner presents options to a husband and wife for their daughter's wedding.

170. PLAYFUL/LETHARGIC/APATHETIC

A young boy wants his two friends to play a game of hide-and-seek with him.

171. DEFERENTIAL/BRASH/DIPLOMATIC

A newspaper reporter asks two mayoral candidates to explain why voters should support them.

172. EXASPERATED/INATTENTIVE/UNEASY

A teacher gives exam instructions to two students.

173. DESPONDENT/EMOTIONAL/DISPASSIONATE

A beggar on the street shares his life story with two strangers.

174. RESOLUTE/SPINELESS/INDIFFERENT

Three construction workers, dissatisfied with their working conditions, consider walking off the job.

175. PERSUASIVE/COMMITTED/UNDECIDED

An Army Recruiter speaks to two young men about joining the Army.

176. FORCEFUL/RESISTANT/ACQUIESCENT

A police officer searching for prison escapees detains two suspects.

177. REASSURING/DISCOURAGED/FRUSTRATED

A teacher allows two of her students to retake a test they both failed.

178. SYSTEMATIC/HAPHAZARD/DISTRACTED

Three friends work on a jigsaw puzzle together.

179. WELL-INTENTIONED/SELF-INDULGENT/SELF-DENYING

A waiter recommends dessert choices to two diners.

180. BOASTFUL/UNBELIEVING/DERISIVE

A fisherman tells two friends about a huge fish he caught.

181. DISCONCERTED/BITTER/RELIEVED

An office manager fires two long-time employees.

182. JUBILANT/ACERBIC/BLASÉ

A guy standing in a park with two friends identifies different birds for them.

183. FORMIDABLE/CRAVEN/COMBATIVE

A teacher insists that two students sitting in the back row of her classroom pay closer attention.

184. URBANE/UNCOUTH/OBLIVIOUS

The maître d' of an elegant restaurant refuses to seat two improperly dressed patrons.

185. RECKLESS/AUDACIOUS/DISCREET

Two teenagers promise their father that they will behave properly if he gives them permission to go to a party.

186. EARNEST/INFURIATED/DELIGHTED

The manager of an accounting firm tells two job applicants that he can't hire them because their good looks would distract the other workers.

187. PROUD/RESTRAINED/INDISCREET

A father shows pictures of his newborn baby to his two friends.

188. INGRATIATING/SUSPICIOUS/OBLIVIOUS

A boy tells his mother and father that they're the best parents in the world.

189. INTROSPECTIVE/PENSIVE/SHALLOW

Three friends contemplate the meaning of life.

190. STRIDENT/TIRELESS/WEARY

A drill sergeant commands two soldiers to begin a twenty-mile hike.

191. CUNNING/SLOW-WITTED/CAPTIOUS

A prison inmate divulges his escape plan to his two cellmates.

192. INSOLENT/BEFUDDLED/ASTOUNDED

A restaurant diner speaks to his waiter and the restaurant manager about the steak he was just served.

193. CONTRITE/UNSPARING/MERCIFUL

A teenage boy apologizes to his parents for lying to them about his whereabouts the night before.

194. GRUFF/DUBIOUS/UNINTERESTED

A grandfather tells his two grandchildren what it was like growing up when he was young.

195. DETERMINED/OBDURATE/FLEXIBLE

A teenage girl tries to persuade her parents to extend her curfew.

196. FIXATED/NARCISSISTIC/MEEK

A photographer works with two fashion models.

197. INSPIRING/CRITICAL/DOGGED

Two track coaches speak to a runner as he approaches the finish line.

198. INFLUENTIAL/UNCERTAIN/LEERY

A realtor tries to sell an expensive house to a married couple.

199. UPBEAT/FORLORN/AGGRAVATED

A tennis coach speaks to his doubles players after they lose a close match.

200. SUPPORTIVE/OFFENDED/GRATEFUL

A mother tells her two teenage daughters that they'd look better if they wore a little more makeup.

USING OBSTACLES IN SOLO IMPROVISATIONS

The leading characters in a good play or film often need to overcome many difficult obstacles before they can accomplish their objectives. Some of these obstacles may be physical, perhaps involving destructive forces of nature, time limitations, or the interference of others. Others are psychological, perhaps involving deep-seated guilt or hidden fears. Whatever the type, the obstacles help create powerful dramatic tension and excitement.

Each of the one hundred improvisation starters in this chapter provides an obstacle that stands in the way of an objective. The player must find a way to overcome this barrier to her objective. Some obstacles are physical, some are psychological, but all will challenge the player to find a creative solution to his predicament.

The improvisation starters included here are to be performed solo so the player can concentrate on removing his obstruction without the help of another person. This is more difficult to do than improvisation starters for two or more players, as the player must find his own solution to the problem.

These solo improvisations are simple to run. The instructor or moderator should have the player take the stage or playing area and then read the situation aloud to both the player and the audience. The improvisation should then start immediately.

Review the following guidelines before beginning:

- Work on overcoming your obstacle throughout the entire improvisation. Try as many ways as you can think of to do this.

But be warned, you may find yourself in an impossible situation! Keep going until you've overcome your obstacle or your instructor/moderator tells you to stop.

- Don't feel obligated to speak. The improvisation may be performed as a pantomime. Most people don't constantly talk to themselves when they are alone, but some people do like to "think out loud." If thinking out loud helps, then go ahead and do it, but don't do it for the benefit of the audience. If the audience doesn't understand what you're doing, don't worry about it. You can discuss the improvisation with them after it's over.

You may use the following guide questions when discussing the performances with your players and audience:

- How did the player attempt to overcome the obstacle? Was an original approach used?
- Did the player clearly understand the objective?
- What might the player have done differently to overcome the obstacle and accomplish the objective? What do you think you would have done?
- What was the player's attitude toward the obstacle? What was his mood or emotional state?

As in previous chapters, most of the situations do not require gender-specific characters. Feel free to switch male references to female and female references to male.

1. You're driving to a very important job interview, following the directions provided by your car's built-in GPS system. Suddenly, the system unexpectedly shuts down. You have no idea how to get there on your own, and the interview is scheduled to begin very soon.

2. You're cooking a steak dinner for a friend who will arrive shortly. Suddenly, you remember your friend recently decided to follow a strict vegetarian diet. You have one head of lettuce in your re-

frigerator, but other than that, you don't have much else to use to prepare a quick vegetarian meal.

3. Today is your first day on the job as a trainer in a health and fitness club. You're scheduled to teach a full body conditioning class in ten minutes. As you set up the equipment for your class, you pull a muscle in your back while moving some weights. You can hardly move! You don't know how you can teach the class without demonstrating your activities and exercises for your students.

4. You're a college student typing the last sentence of a twenty-page research paper on your laptop, when suddenly your laptop crashes. You try to reboot your laptop, but when you press the power key, nothing happens! It's late at night and the paper needs to be submitted early in the morning, and you haven't saved a backup of the paper on any other device.

5. You've just finished eating a meal at a restaurant. You reach into your pocket for your wallet and discover it's missing. You suddenly remember you left it on your kitchen table at home. You have no cash or credit cards on you, and the waitress will deliver your check in a few minutes.

6. You're a house painter who has just completed painting the interior of a house. While checking your invoice, you realize you painted all the moldings the wrong color! The homeowners will be back any minute to inspect your work.

7. Your neighbor's dog has been staying at your house with you while they've been away on vacation. They'll be at your house within the hour to pick him up. You decide to walk the dog one more time before they arrive, but when you call the dog's name, he doesn't come to you. It's then that you notice a large hole in the screen door leading to the outside of your house. The dog has disappeared!

8. This morning your neighbor asked you to feed her cat while she is away for the day. She gave you a key to her house, but when you open the front door, the house alarm sounds. Apparently, she forgot to disable it, and you don't know the code to turn it off. The police will be there in a few seconds.

9. It's late at night. You're a student studying for test you will take in the morning, but you're very sleepy and struggling to stay awake. You need to review the material in order to pass the test, and you need to pass the test in order to pass the course.

10. You're a newspaper photographer. Your assignment today is to photograph the grand opening of a beautiful new shopping mall. As you're taking your first picture, your camera slips out of your hand and the lens shatters. You don't have another lens, and your editor needs the photos within the hour.

11. You're throwing a huge party at your house. Guests will arrive shortly. The caterer was supposed to deliver and set up food trays a half-hour ago, but they have yet to appear. Panicking, you call the caterer and find out their kitchen caught fire last night, and therefore they were unable to prepare your food.

12. You woke up this morning feeling awful. You don't know how you're going to drag yourself to work, but you've already taken all your allotted sick days this year. You're afraid that if you don't go in today, you will be fired.

13. While your roommate is away on vacation, you'd like to take advantage of the time she's gone by disposing of all her cheap and ugly tchotchkes that clutter the apartment. You're not sure how she will respond when she sees they're gone, but you just can't stand having these things around anymore.

14. You recently purchased a new cellphone from an overseas vendor at an incredibly low price. When the package arrives, you open it and find that the instruction manual is written entirely in Japanese. You have no idea how to activate the phone.

15. You are the guest of honor at a party tonight. Hundreds of people will be there. Just as you're about to leave for the party, your phone rings. It's your boss, and he needs you to cover a shift tonight. Your boss has not been too happy with you lately, and you're afraid that if you deny his request, you will be fired.

16. You've been working late into the night to finish a project that's due tomorrow. No one else is in the office. You take a break to go to the bathroom, but when you try to leave, you discover the door has been locked and doesn't open from the inside. Apparently, a custodian thought the bathroom was empty and locked the door. You left your cell phone on your desk.

17. You're standing outside your boss's office, trying to decide whether to knock on his door and tell him you quit. You hate your job, and the thought of continuing another day doing it makes you sick; however, your job pays quite well, and you don't think you will ever find another job that pays nearly as much.

18. You're ice skating on a frozen lake when you see a fellow skater fall through the ice. As you approach the skater flailing his arms helplessly in the freezing-cold water, the ice beneath you starts to crack. If you move any further, you might break through the ice yourself.

19. Your wife Lara always wanted you to have a tattoo applied to your chest that reads "I Love Lara," and you decided to have it done today. But when you return home, you notice that it says "I Love Dara." Apparently, the tattoo artist misunderstood you. Coincidentally, Dara is the name of an ex-girlfriend. Lara is anxious to see the tattoo, and she will be home any minute.

20. You've decided it's time to leave the comfort of your parents' home and venture out on your own, but you don't know whether to buy your own place or rent. You're pretty sure you can afford a mortgage, but you wouldn't have much disposable cash available. On the other hand, you feel that paying rent is like throwing money away. You decide to take out a sheet of paper and list the advantages and disadvantages of buying vs. renting.

21. You're a private investigator who's been assigned to take photos of a man whose wife believes he has been cheating on her. You've found the man inside the lobby of an expensive hotel with a strange woman and immediately take out your camera. Trying to be as inconspicuous as possible, you begin to take photos of the two of them, but the man notices you. He looks angry.

22. You're filling out an application for a job you want badly. You know you will have a better chance of getting hired if you indicate on the application that you have a college degree; however, you never completed college. You're considering lying on the application and stating you graduated college, hoping the prospective employer will not request a college transcript.

23. You are watching a war movie. The sight of blood makes you swoon, but you are completely absorbed in the film and want to see every second of it. It appears that a very bloody battle scene is about to begin.

24. You're housesitting for your friend while he is away. However, before he left, your friend neglected to tell you that he just adopted a cat. He left you a note asking that you feed and care for it. You are highly allergic to cats.

25. You've just had some dental work done, and your mouth is still numb from the anesthetic. The dentist told you not to eat anything for at least a few hours, but you're starving! There's a fast-food restaurant just outside the dentist's office.

26. Your friend called to ask if you're interested in golfing with him today. You'd love to go, but you promised your wife that you'd help her clean the house today. You're considering asking your

wife if she'd mind if you went golfing today instead of cleaning, but you think she might become upset with you if you did.

27. You're in the cereal aisle of a supermarket, searching for your favorite breakfast cereal. Small children are running up and down the aisle, screaming and pulling boxes off the shelves. The children's mother is chatting on her cellphone and totally ignoring her unruly children. You're thinking about politely speaking to the mother about her children's poor behavior, but you're not sure how she will respond and you don't want to make a bad situation even worse.

28. You're a high school senior who's just received a college acceptance letter. Lately, you've been thinking about traveling around the world for a year or two before starting college; however, you don't think your parents will approve of that plan. You need to make a decision soon.

29. You're sitting in an airport terminal waiting for your flight to start boarding when you notice a woman carrying an expensive handbag that looks exactly like one that was stolen from you last week. You're thinking about creating a distraction so you can get a closer look and see if it's yours.

30. You found the perfect makeup product for your skin! However, it costs ten times as much as you care to spend on makeup, and you're a little strapped for cash right now.

31. Yesterday, a co-worker asked you out on a date, and you told him you need some time to think about it. You like the guy very much, but you're afraid of the potential problems of dating a co-worker. He's expecting an answer today.

32. You're at a racetrack, and you've just received a tip on a horse from a very reputable source. You just got paid today, and you're considering betting your entire paycheck on this horse. How-

ever, if the horse doesn't finish first, you won't be able to pay your bills this month.

33. You're driving to work, and you're running late. Last week, your boss told you that if you're late one more time, you will be fired. You start to accelerate when you notice a police car is behind you. You already have a number of speeding tickets, and if you get one more, you will lose your license.

34. You're a politician about to give a very important speech to a group of financial supporters. You're standing in the wings, drinking a cup of coffee and waiting to be introduced. Just as your name is announced, you accidentally spill coffee all over your suit and shirt.

35. You're sitting in front of your computer, looking at some embarrassing pictures of yourself from when you were two years old that your mother posted on Facebook. You'd like to call your mother and tell her to stop posting embarrassing photos of you, but you know her feelings will be hurt if you do. She clearly thinks the photos are adorable.

36. Your marriage is not going well, and you are considering asking your spouse for a divorce. There are children and finances to consider, and you're not sure how your spouse will react when you bring up the subject. You need to think this through very carefully.

37. You're an investment advisor. One of your clients had asked you to invest in a particular stock for him last week. Without telling him, you bought one hundred shares of a different stock that you thought would make him a lot more money. Unfortunately, during the week, shares in the stock you bought sank miserably, while the stock your client asked you to buy climbed significantly. In a few minutes, your client will be at your office to review his portfolio.

38. Yesterday, you interviewed for two jobs, and today you found out you were offered both positions. One job pays much more than the other, but you like the lower-paying job much better. You need to call both employers back today with your decision.

39. You met someone really great on an online dating service. Your date wants to go to a karaoke bar on your first date because you indicated in your online bio that you're a terrific singer. Truthfully, you have a horrible singing voice. You never thought you'd be asked to sing.

40. Recently, you lost a great amount of weight. Tonight, you're attending a very formal event, and as you prepare to dress for it, you realize your only formal suit is about three sizes too big for you. There isn't time to go out and buy another one.

41. You come home at 2 A.M. after a very long night, when you realize your house keys are locked inside the house. As you pry open a window and climb into the house, a police officer on patrol approaches you. You also left your ID inside the house and can't prove you live there.

42. You just found out that you won big money in a contest sponsored by a radio station. You have exactly five minutes to call the station to claim your prize. As you enter the number into your mobile phone, the battery dies, and you can't remember where you left the charger. There's no other phone available.

43. Working as an electrician's assistant, you've been asked to hang an expensive chandelier. As you connect the chandelier's wires to the electrical box in the ceiling, the chandelier slips out of your hands and shatters into pieces on the ground. Your boss will arrive any second to inspect your work.

44. You're a bartender setting up for the evening crowd. The special drink for the night is a margarita, and you know lots of people will be ordering them. As you check the back bar, you notice there's only one half-filled bottle of tequila left. (Tequila is the main ingredient in a margarita.) Apparently, the manager didn't order enough tequila this week. The bar will open in a few minutes.

45. You have the day off from work. You promised your wife that you would clean and straighten up around the house today while she's at work because she's bringing friends over for dinner. Unfortunately, you forgot about your promise and the house is a mess. She will be home with the dinner guests at any moment.

46. You bought an expensive crystal vase yesterday. This morning, you decided that you didn't like it and want to return it. As you pick it up to put it in its box, it slips from your hand, falls to the ground, and shatters into pieces.

47. Your boss just called to tell you that he needs you to go on a business trip halfway across the country this weekend. When you were hired, you didn't think you'd be sent on business trips. You haven't told your boss, but you're deathly afraid of flying.

48. You have a date tonight, and you're considering going on the date without any makeup. You hate that it takes so much time to put it on and take it off; however, you like how you look when you're all made up. Your date will be picking you up in a couple of hours, so you need to make a decision soon.

49. Your daughter's class is expecting her to bring homemade cookies to class. Last night, you promised to make them for her, but unfortunately, you forgot! She needs to leave in five minutes to get to school on time.

50. Your beloved pet dog suffered an injury that requires expensive surgery, and your veterinarian can't guarantee the surgery will be successful. Your options are to go ahead with the surgery and hope for the best or to have the dog euthanized. You are already thousands of dollars in debt and can hardly afford the operation.

51. You make a living as a hand model, and you have a modeling job later in the day. Last night, you accidentally hit your hand with a hammer while hanging pictures on a wall, and your hand is badly bruised. If you cancel the job, you will lose thousands of dollars.

52. You're a competitive ice skater, and today you're skating for a championship medal. As you're leaving for the competition, you trip over something outside your house and sprain your ankle.

53. You're filling your bathtub with water when you notice the drain is clogged. You don't have a plunger or anything else readily available to clear the drain. Your only option is to shut off the water and call a plumber, but when you do, the faucet handle snaps off and the water continues to flow! You have no idea where the main shutoff valve is located.

54. You're at the funeral of a friend. Although you are very sad that he has passed, you begin to remember how funny he was. You recall one particular incident that has always made you laugh out loud, and right now you're struggling to keep your composure thinking about it. It would be inappropriate to burst out laughing.

55. You're a teenager. It's late at night and you are out with your friends. You lost track of time and now it's well past your curfew. You know your parents will be very upset with you.

56. The battery on your mobile phone died, so you borrowed a friend's phone to make an important call. You're not familiar with his phone, and while trying to make the call, you accidently delete all of his contact information.

57. Guests have arrived at your house for a wine-and-cheese party. You're ready to open a bottle of wine and start pouring, but you can't seem to find a corkscrew!

58. Your husband wants to start a family, but you're not ready. You've been taking birth control pills to avoid getting pregnant, but you've kept it a secret from your husband because you're afraid of how he might react if you told him the truth. Today, you've decided you need to be honest about both the pills and the fact that you don't want to have a baby just yet, but you're not sure how to do it.

59. You just e-mailed copies of your résumé to a few potential employers. After sending them, you noticed that you mistakenly sent a first draft of it instead of the final version. The first draft is filled with typos and spelling errors.

60. You're getting ready to report to your first day of work as a server in a restaurant. Yesterday, you were given a special shirt you're required to wear, but you never thought to try it on until now. It turns out that the shirt you were given is extra small, and your size is large. Your shift begins in twenty minutes.

61. Your sister and your closest friend are getting married, and both would like you to be their maid of honor. Unfortunately, the two weddings will take place on the same day, and circumstances beyond their control prevent either from changing the date. You need to choose one over the other.

62. You're a server in a restaurant. When you got to work today, your manager told you the bartender called in sick and he needs you to fill in. When you told him that you had no idea how to mix drinks, he said, "Do your best" and walked away. The restaurant opens in ten minutes.

63. You're a construction worker. You've just finished cutting one hundred 6-foot lengths of 2" × 4" lumber for the foreman. After removing the last piece from the workbench, you check the construction plans and see that all one hundred pieces were supposed to be 8 feet in length! The foreman will arrive in a few minutes.

64. You're a landscaper, and you just finished planting a large number of expensive shrubs and flowers in a client's garden while he's away on vacation. Now you need to water them, but when you turn on the exterior water faucet, nothing comes out of the hose. It seems the homeowner has turned off the water from the inside of his house, and all the doors to the house are locked. It's a very hot day, and if you don't water these plants soon, they will die. The homeowner will not return until tomorrow.

65. You're watching a football game, and your team is winning! Every time they score or make a good play, you want to cheer loudly, but you're surrounded by angry fans of the other team. Rooting for your team might be dangerous!

66. You're in a shoe store. You've been looking for a certain style of shoe for quite a while now, and you finally see exactly what you've been looking for! You try them on, but unfortunately, they are just a bit too small and they aren't available in a larger size. You could wear them, but they'd be very uncomfortable. You don't see anything else you like.

67. You're alone in the wilderness on a camping trip, waiting for friends to join you. You told them you'd have a roaring fire going and a meal prepared before they arrived. You try starting a fire, but it had rained the night before and all the firewood that you laid out is soaking wet, making it impossible for you to ignite the logs. Your friends will be arriving shortly.

68. You're getting dressed to go out on a date with a very special person. You've been anticipating this date for a long time. As you bend over to tie your shoes, you throw out your back and can't move! You're afraid that if you cancel this date, you'll never have another chance.

69. Yesterday, your friend gave you five dollars and asked you to buy a lottery ticket for him. This morning, you learned that the ticket you bought is a winner worth a million dollars! Your friend doesn't know which numbers you picked for him. He'll be over to pick up the ticket any minute. It would be very easy for you to just tell him you forgot to buy the ticket and give him back his five dollars.

70. You're alone in your house reading a book when you hear a noise in an adjacent room. You believe someone has broken into your house. You try calling the police, but it seems the landline in your house has been disconnected and your cellphone battery is dead.

71. You're a teenager whose parents asked you to make a list of people you would like to invite to a birthday party they're throwing for you next week. You have a crude, obnoxious uncle you can't stand, but for some reason, your parents love him and would be upset if he weren't included on the list. You're struggling to decide whether or not to add him to the list.

72. You have a temporary job working in a factory. Most of your fellow workers have decided to go on strike until the factory owner agrees to offer them higher wages. You believe you are paid a fair wage and don't want to participate in the strike; however, you don't want to be labeled a scab.

73. You borrowed your friend's expensive car, promising to be very careful with it. As you turn onto your friend's street to return the car, another car runs a stop sign and hits your friend's fender. You're okay, but the car is badly damaged.

74. You're meeting your wife tonight for her mother's birthday party. Your wife just called from work to remind you to bring the cake that she specially made for her mother. You didn't realize the cake was for the party and ate half of it during the day!

75. You're absorbed in watching an exciting movie on television when you realize you need to get to an important appointment. You try pulling yourself away from the television, but you can't seem to move.

76. You're a single man sitting at a bar alone when an attractive woman walks into the bar and sits in the empty seat beside you. You'd like to introduce yourself and buy the woman a drink, but your level of self-confidence is low. The last time you asked a woman on a date, you were badly rejected.

77. You own a small boutique. Your husband begged you to hire his sister as a salesperson, and you obliged. However, she's proven to be lazy and incompetent, so you fired her. You're certain your husband will be upset when you tell him; you're trying to decide how to break the news to him.

78. It's the morning of your wedding anniversary, and your spouse seems to have forgotten. You'd like to express your anger, but you have your pride.

79. You're suffering a painful shoulder injury, and your doctor told you it was very important to take your prescribed pain pills twice a day, but no more than twice a day. It's late at night and you're about to go to bed, but you can't remember whether or not you took a second pill earlier in the day. You certainly don't want to overdose on the medication, but you're in extreme pain.

80. You've decided you want to break up with your girlfriend, but you can't stand the thought of telling her in person. You're thinking of sending her a breakup text, but you know that everyone will accuse you of being a coward.

81. It's late at night and you're trying to get to sleep, but your roommate is blasting loud rock music in the next room. You have an important meeting at work early the next morning, and you need to be sharp. You'd normally just get up and tell him to turn it down, but your car is broken and you need him to drive you to work in the morning. You're afraid that if you say anything to him, he won't do it.

82. Your coworkers are planning a retirement party for your boss, and they want you to contribute toward a gift. They all love the boss, but you've always had personal reasons for hating her. You never let anyone know your true feelings because you didn't want to be considered a malcontent. You know you'd be betraying yourself if you offered even a dime, but if you finally admit why you don't want to contribute, your co-workers will realize that you've been a phony and lose any respect they might have had for you.

83. You've bragged to your friends about how much weight you can lift when you work out at the gym. In reality, you really can't lift nearly as much as you say you can. You're at the gym now, and a friend has just sent you a text message saying he's just outside the door of the gym and is about to come inside to watch you lift. You have no escape!

84. You just climbed up a very tall ladder and stepped onto the roof of your house to repair some broken shingles. Suddenly, the ladder falls to the ground. The roof is too high for you to consider jumping off. You live on a dead-end street, and no one is around. You also left your mobile phone inside the house.

85. You're a model at a fashion show. One minute before you're scheduled to step out onto the runway, you realize you're wearing the wrong outfit. If the designer of the outfit that you're supposed to be wearing sees you in the wrong outfit, you will certainly lose your job with your modeling agency.

86. You were selected to buy lottery tickets for your office lottery pool. Your boss and a dozen co-workers are depending on you. When you get to the store to buy them, you realize that you forgot to take the cash you collected from everyone and you don't have any personal cash with you. The store doesn't accept credit cards or checks for lottery ticket purchases. The drawing will take place in a few minutes.

87. You just found a wallet lying on the sidewalk that has five hundred dollars in cash inside it. You know the right thing to do is turn the wallet in to the nearest police station, but you just lost your job and you desperately need the money.

88. You're preparing a romantic dinner for you and your girlfriend. While striking a match to light a candle on the dinner table, the entire matchbox catches fire and falls on the table, and the tablecloth bursts into flames. You grab a fire extinguisher, but when you pull the pin to operate it, you discover it's empty.

89. You have a very bad toothache and need to see a dentist, but you're very afraid of dentists. You try to convince yourself that the pain will subside by itself, but it just seems to be getting worse. You're not sure how much pain you can endure before you break down and make an appointment with a dentist.

90. Today is your ten-year-old child's birthday. You promised your child a new bicycle as a birthday present. The bicycle was shipped to you this morning unassembled. You search the box for assembly instructions, but you can't find any. You're not very good with your hands, and besides that, you don't own any tools. You had planned to give your child the bicycle this afternoon.

91. You're a roadie for a famous rock band, and it's your job to tune the lead guitarist's guitar. Just before a concert is about to begin, the guitar slips out of your hands and its neck breaks in half. It's the guitarist's favorite, and he wants to use it for the opening number.

92. You've invited your boss to your home for a cocktail, and he will be arriving at any moment. You know he only drinks top-shelf scotch, but when you check your liquor cabinet, you notice your bottle of expensive scotch is empty! You're considering filling the bottle with cheap scotch and hoping he can't tell the difference.

93. You borrowed money from a friend last week and promised you'd pay him back today. Unfortunately, you gambled the money away in a poker game last night and you're completely broke. Your friend needs the money today to cover some bills.

94. You're trying to open a jar of peanut butter, but you're having a great deal of trouble twisting off the lid. You've tried running it underwater and tapping the side of the lid with a spoon, but you still can't open it. You need to develop a new strategy.

95. You're dining alone in a restaurant. The waiter hands you a menu, but the print is very small and difficult to read. You left your reading glasses at home.

96. You've just come home from the dermatologist's office after being treated for exposure to poison ivy. The doctor told you not to scratch the infected area because that may irritate the skin further or worsen the infection. You were given anti-itch lotion to apply, but it doesn't seem to be working. You want to scratch yourself badly!

97. Your friends have been telling you that you need to exercise more. You reluctantly promised them you'd go for a long run with them today; however, you just can't seem to motivate yourself to do it, and you're trying to come up with an excuse they'll accept.

98. Ever since you were a child, you've had the ability to communicate with the dead. You've always kept your gift to yourself out of fear that people would think you're crazy or weird. Now that psychic mediums are becoming more accepted, you're considering telling others about your gift, but you still fear the reaction you might get.

99. You're a high school student trying to decide whether or not to pretend you're sick so your parents will let you stay home from school. You don't want to go to school because you're not prepared to take a math test today; however, if your parents find out you faked an illness to avoid a test, there will be hell to pay.

100. Your friends want you to take an improvisation class with them, but you're not sure you'd enjoy it. You have the application for the class in your hand and are debating whether or not to complete it and mail it in.

USING LINES OF DIALOGUE

Many beginning actors don't know how to listen—onstage, that is. They receive their scripts, memorize their lines, and try to perfect the exact way each line will be delivered. Once they decide which specific vocal inflections and facial expressions work best, they make sure each line comes across exactly the same way for every single performance. After a while, it is no longer necessary to listen to the other actors onstage. As long as they recognize their cues, they're safe. Why bother worrying about an honest response to another character on stage when you've already figured out the perfect way to deliver your lines?

Obviously, real life doesn't work this way. We respond to more than just words; we respond to the *way* words are spoken. If someone were to call you an idiot, you might become very angry, or you might laugh—it all depends on your perception of the person's tone of voice and visible expression.

Theater, of course, is a reflection of real life. If the audience of a play sensed the characters weren't really listening to each other, they might not be so willing to *suspend their disbelief* and view the play as a reality.

One of the reasons acting instructors use improvisation is to teach the actor to listen. Since no words or actions have been prepared ahead of time, the actor *must* listen in order to respond. The improvisation starters in this chapter force the player to listen very carefully to how the other player in the scene delivers the opening line, since that line will determine how she will react. She will be compelled to respond not only to the *words* she hears but also to the meaning *behind* the words.

This chapter is divided into two sections. The first section includes one hundred single lines of dialogue that will serve as the first line spoken in the improvisation. Simply have your players take the stage, choose a line, and whisper it to one of the players. *The other player should not know the line in advance.* The scene begins when the first player delivers the line. The second player should pay close attention to the first player's visible and vocal expression and tailor her response to align with the way the opening line is spoken. Character relationships, objectives, and motivations will most likely become clear early in the scene. The players can end the scene themselves after they feel they've reached their objectives or exhausted the possibilities for reaching them, or the instructor can signal them to stop after a predetermined amount of time.

The second section includes one hundred pairs of opening and closing lines. To run these improvisations, have two players take the stage and whisper the opening line to the first player and the closing line to the second player. *The players should not know each other's lines in advance.* Once the first player speaks the opening line, the second player should respond *with something other than his assigned closing line.* The conversation should continue until the second player is motivated to use his closing line to end the scene.

Before the second player responds to the first player's opening line, it's important that he keeps in mind his assigned closing line, since it will determine the direction of the scene. For example, if the first player's opening line is "I have a problem," and the second player's closing line is "Problem solved," the second player knows he must say and do things during the course of the improv that will logically lead toward a resolution. Once the closing line is spoken, the second player should say "Scene!" to end the improvisation.

Note: The player with the first line of dialogue doesn't necessarily have to begin speaking immediately. Some silent action may precede the line. For example, if the opening line were "This place is a mess," the player might look around at the condition of the room for a while before speaking. However, the other actor must not say anything until the line is spoken.

You may use the following questions to guide your discussion of the performances:

- How would you describe the first player's tone of voice, attitude, emotional state, or mood when he spoke the opening line?
- Were you surprised by the second player's response to the first line? Why or why not? Would you have responded in a similar way?
- What kind of obstacles faced each player?
- Do you think the first player delivered the opening line in the most conventional way? How could the line have been delivered differently to evoke a different response from the second player?
- Describe the overall mood of the scene.

Single Lines

Two Players

1. You're under arrest.

2. I wish it would stop raining.

3. I can tell by your silence that something is terribly wrong.

4. Sometimes I wish I could just disappear.

5. I can't believe I finally have the chance to meet you!

6. We have absolutely nothing in common.

7. Why don't you just admit that you're a liar and a cheater?

8. Why are you so frightened?

9. Have you ever seen a more beautiful sky?

10. Blue just isn't your color.

11. You're not very bright, are you?

12. Can our luck get any worse?

13. Do you hear those voices?

14. I'm not leaving until you admit the truth.

15. So, how do you really feel about me?

16. Do these jeans make me look fat?

17. I came here to tell you that I'm broke.

18. Frankly, I don't care what you think.

19. I think you've had too much to drink.

20. Sometimes you just have to know when to give up.

21. Let's play truth or dare.

22. What's that smell?

23. I'm reading your mind right now.

24. So what's the plan?

25. I don't think you're ready.

26. If I were your boss, I'd fire you.

27. I have no idea where we are right now.

28. Has anyone ever told you that less is more?

29. If you want a friend, be a friend.

30. Most of what I've told you about myself is a lie.

31. Why don't you ever take me seriously?

32. You're not the person I thought you were.

33. I am so incredibly proud of you!

34. I'm sorry, but I just can't forgive you.

35. This is going to be so much fun!

36. Do you think I should take singing lessons?

37. It's not you, it's me.

38. Another year has passed, and nothing is different.

39. Let's get a puppy!

40. I was born to be wild.

41. Maybe we should just go our separate ways.

42. You're the last person I thought I'd find here!

43. I'm starving.

44. Dreams really can come true!

45. Why are you alone?

46. What did you want to speak to me about?

47. I knew I'd find you here!

48. We need to settle this once and for all.

49. Isn't there any place I can go to be alone?

50. You're not going to believe who I saw.

51. So … I heard you won the lottery!

52. Where's your friend?

53. Why have you been ignoring me?

54. My car won't start.

55. I believe you owe me an explanation.

56. Do you want to go out for dinner with me this weekend?

57. Did you get a haircut?

58. I've decided to go on a long trip.

59. I think the police know what we did.

60. Thank you for the flowers!

61. I appreciate your offer, but I don't need your help.

62. You started this, but I'm going to end it.

63. Would you care to dance?

64. I've been thinking about what you asked, and I've decided I must say no.

65. Are you finished?

66. What's the meaning of that text message you sent me last night?

67. Looks like it's just you and me.

68. You need to leave immediately!

69. I'm so glad to have you on my side.

70. I need the money you owe me.

71. So much to do, so little time.

72. I'm not interested in your excuses.

73. What planet are you from?

74. I'm going to tell you something, but I don't want you to judge me.

75. Perhaps it's time we both went on a diet.

Three Players

76. I'm pretty sure one of you is lying.

77. I'm sorry, but I can only take one of you with me.

78. I'm here to help you two settle your argument.

79. There's no way you two are related.

80. One of you is the winner, and the other must go home.

81. I know you two are going out on a date tonight, but do you mind if I tag along?

82. Which one of you took the last doughnut?

83. So … you didn't have the guts to show up alone, did you?

84. Do you really think I'm going to say which one of you I like better?

85. Why did you bring him along with you?

86. Do either one of you want my extra ticket for the concert tonight?

87. I hate to do this, but I'm going to have to fire one of you.

88. I want to know the secret you two have been keeping from me.

89. Is this the person you've been seeing behind my back?

90. I have good news for one of you and bad news for the other.

91. I can tell the two of you love each other.

92. I hate that you two aren't speaking to each other.

93. I think we all know which one of us isn't doing his fair share.

94. Who wants to sit in the middle?

95. Can one of you drive me to the airport?

96. What were you two just whispering about?

97. One of you can stay, but the other needs to leave.

98. Have you two decided whether or not to go into business together?

99. There's only enough left for two of us.

100. Are you two getting divorced?

Opening and Closing Lines for Two Players

1. OPENING LINE: Are you sure we should do this?
CLOSING LINE: We're lucky to have made it through that alive!

2. OPENING LINE: I think I've discovered the meaning of life!
CLOSING LINE: Maybe you shouldn't try to think so much.

3. OPENING LINE: I don't have a very good feeling about this place.
CLOSING LINE: I think we learned a very important lesson today.

4. OPENING LINE: I'm hungry and tired, and I want to go home.
CLOSING LINE: Aren't you glad you stayed?

5. OPENING LINE: Oh come on, don't be a little baby.
CLOSING LINE: My mother is going to throw a fit!

6. OPENING LINE: I'm sorry. Do I know you?
CLOSING LINE: I feel like a complete fool.

7. OPENING LINE: I'm not going to take any more of your crap.
CLOSING LINE: Maybe we should call a truce.

8. OPENING LINE: I know exactly where we are.
CLOSING LINE: If I don't return by midnight, send out a search party.

9. OPENING LINE: What if we try pushing this button?
CLOSING LINE: There! Now it works perfectly!

10. OPENING LINE: We can't go on like this anymore.
CLOSING LINE: Sometimes it's best to just start over.

11. **OPENING LINE:** This is where I last saw him.
    CLOSING LINE: Maybe we should come back again tomorrow.

12. **OPENING LINE:** Just sit there and don't move!
    CLOSING LINE: Don't forget about me!

13. **OPENING LINE:** You think you know all the answers, don't you?
    CLOSING LINE: I hope you learned your lesson.

14. **OPENING LINE:** Something tells me we're in the wrong place.
    CLOSING LINE: That was pretty funny!

15. **OPENING LINE:** You appear to be lost.
    CLOSING LINE: Can you explain that to me again?

16. **OPENING LINE:** That looks so good!
    CLOSING LINE: Appearances are often deceiving.

17. **OPENING LINE:** Have you ever seen a sky so blue?
    CLOSING LINE: Wow! I never saw that coming!

18. **OPENING LINE:** If you love me, let me go.
    CLOSING LINE: You just proved my point.

19. **OPENING LINE:** We need to do this my way!
    CLOSING LINE: I stand corrected.

20. **OPENING LINE:** All we need is the air we breathe.
    CLOSING LINE: You're so naïve.

21. **OPENING LINE:** How are we ever going to know if we don't try?
    CLOSING LINE: Sometimes it's better just to give up.

22. **OPENING LINE:** Want to hear a joke?
    CLOSING LINE: Don't quit your day job.

23. **OPENING LINE:** When I woke up this morning, I knew it was going to be a terrible day.
    CLOSING LINE: Hope springs eternal.

24. OPENING LINE: I have a great idea!
CLOSING LINE: Well, it was worth a try.

25. OPENING LINE: Okay, we're here. Now what?
CLOSING LINE: I don't know how I stayed awake through that.

26. OPENING LINE: What are you doing here?
CLOSING LINE: Sorry to have bothered you.

27. OPENING LINE: What should we do with this?
CLOSING LINE: We'd better get out of here.

28. OPENING LINE: Should we give this one more try?
CLOSING LINE: My only regret is that we didn't try this sooner.

29. OPENING LINE: You're the last person on Earth I expected to see today.
CLOSING LINE: I just don't think this is going to work out.

30. OPENING LINE: What is that ridiculous thing you're wearing?
CLOSING LINE: Maybe you're right.

31. OPENING LINE: If you give me one more chance, I know I can make this work.
CLOSING LINE: Some things are just better left unsaid.

32. OPENING LINE: I have just as much a right to be here as you do.
CLOSING LINE: I'm glad we worked this out.

33. OPENING LINE: So just what is the problem you have with me?
CLOSING LINE: Perhaps I've said too much.

34. OPENING LINE: I just can't stop staring at that.
CLOSING LINE: We've got to get out of here.

35. OPENING LINE: Oh no! It's you again!
CLOSING LINE: So maybe we can be friends after all.

36. OPENING LINE: This is extremely frustrating!
CLOSING LINE: Let's give it another try tomorrow.

37. **OPENING LINE:** I'm beginning to think no one else is going to show up.

    CLOSING LINE: Wait a minute! What day is today?

38. **OPENING LINE:** So what do you think? Should I give it one more try?

    CLOSING LINE: Maybe it's time to give up.

39. **OPENING LINE:** I'm totally exhausted!

    CLOSING LINE: If you give up now, you'll regret it for the rest of your life.

40. **OPENING LINE:** I'm sorry, but I still don't understand.

    CLOSING LINE: I'm losing my patience with you!

41. **OPENING LINE:** Ah! I've been waiting for you!

    CLOSING LINE: I'm sorry. I don't think I can help you.

42. **OPENING LINE:** What's done is done.

    CLOSING LINE: Don't worry. I can fix this.

43. **OPENING LINE:** You have no clue what you're talking about.

    CLOSING LINE: Fine! I'm outta here!

44. **OPENING LINE:** I think I know exactly what's bothering you.

    CLOSING LINE: Thanks. I feel much better now.

45. **OPENING LINE:** I suppose you're wondering why I asked you to meet me here.

    CLOSING LINE: Sorry. I'll never do it again.

46. **OPENING LINE:** Help! I need a place to hide!

    CLOSING LINE: Good luck!

47. **OPENING LINE:** I don't think you understand the mess we're in.

    CLOSING LINE: See that! There's nothing to worry about!

48. **OPENING LINE:** I have no idea what I'm doing.

    CLOSING LINE: Next time, read the manual!

49. OPENING LINE: Are you sure you know what you're doing?
   CLOSING LINE: Maybe I should start over.

50. OPENING LINE: I lost my job today.
   CLOSING LINE: Tomorrow is a new day.

51. OPENING LINE: I had a very strange dream last night.
   CLOSING LINE: I think you might be insane.

52. OPENING LINE: Can I tell you a secret?
   CLOSING LINE: Your secret is safe with me.

53. OPENING LINE: I want a divorce!
   CLOSING LINE: I can't believe this is happening to me!

54. OPENING LINE: What did you want to see me about?
   CLOSING LINE: I have pictures to prove it!

55. OPENING LINE: Please … I just need a little more time.
   CLOSING LINE: I hope you understand how serious I am.

56. OPENING LINE: Hey! You look really great today!
   CLOSING LINE: Sorry, but I'm just not interested.

57. OPENING LINE: What's wrong with the way I'm dressed?
   CLOSING LINE: Are you sure it's supposed to fit like that?

58. OPENING LINE: You owe me an apology.
   CLOSING LINE: Okay, okay … I'm sorry.

59. OPENING LINE: Excuse me, do you need help?
   CLOSING LINE: Thank you! I don't know what I would have done without your help.

60. OPENING LINE: You don't look like the picture I saw online.
   CLOSING LINE: Well, then maybe you should just leave!

61. OPENING LINE: What are you afraid of?
   CLOSING LINE: I guess that wasn't so difficult after all.

62. OPENING LINE: You'll never believe what I heard last night!
CLOSING LINE: Okay, enough! I don't want to hear anymore!

63. OPENING LINE: I'm not leaving until I get a straight answer from you.
CLOSING LINE: Sorry, but that's all I can tell you!

64. OPENING LINE: Did you see that?
CLOSING LINE: Well, that's something you don't see every day.

65. OPENING LINE: I need your advice about something.
CLOSING LINE: Hope that helps.

66. OPENING LINE: I'm so happy this is finally over!
CLOSING LINE: Let's go celebrate!

67. OPENING LINE: There you are! I've been looking all over for you!
CLOSING LINE: And that's why I haven't been around.

68. OPENING LINE: Is what they're saying about you true?
CLOSING LINE: Don't believe everything you hear.

69. OPENING LINE: You're an absolutely amazing person!
CLOSING LINE: It was really no big deal.

70. OPENING LINE: Don't take this the wrong way, but I've got to be honest with you.
CLOSING LINE: Keep your opinion to yourself!

71. OPENING LINE: I think I've had too much to drink.
CLOSING LINE: Why don't you let me drive you home?

72. OPENING LINE: I'm so jealous of you!
CLOSING LINE: I can't believe how great everything turned out!

73. OPENING LINE: The time has finally come for us to leave this place.
CLOSING LINE: We've certainly had some great times here, haven't we?

74. OPENING LINE: Why can't you look me in the eye?

CLOSING LINE: I hope someday you'll be able to forgive me.

75. OPENING LINE: Look, last night I said some things I didn't mean.

CLOSING LINE: Let's just forget last night ever happened.

76. OPENING LINE: Watch this.

CLOSING LINE: Let's never do that again.

77. OPENING LINE: Dinner is ready.

CLOSING LINE: What's for dessert?

78. OPENING LINE: You've become a completely different person.

CLOSING LINE: I guess this is goodbye.

79. OPENING LINE: What a great day for a picnic!

CLOSING LINE: I think I felt a few raindrops.

80. OPENING LINE: Have we met before?

CLOSING LINE: Well, it was nice meeting you.

81. OPENING LINE: I know what you did yesterday.

CLOSING LINE: I'm telling you, that wasn't me!

82. OPENING LINE: Thank God you're here!

CLOSING LINE: Don't worry. Everything is going to be fine.

83. OPENING LINE: I'm sorry, but you're going to have to leave.

CLOSING LINE: Okay, but I'll be back.

84. OPENING LINE: This certainly isn't what I expected.

CLOSING LINE: What a disappointment!

85. OPENING LINE: So what's it going to be? Yes or no?

CLOSING LINE: I'll get back to you tomorrow.

86. OPENING LINE: I can't believe you never told me you were married!

CLOSING LINE: Relax. No one else has to know.

87. OPENING LINE: So … you've come crawling back to me!

CLOSING LINE: I'll just grab my things and leave.

88. OPENING LINE: Shhh! Listen! Do you hear that?

CLOSING LINE: I think you're losing your mind.

89. OPENING LINE: How much money do you have on you?

CLOSING LINE: Easy come, easy go.

90. OPENING LINE: It's freezing cold in this room!

CLOSING LINE: Oh no! I think it's broken.

91. OPENING LINE: If I promise not to bother you, may I stay here for a while?

CLOSING LINE: That's it! Please leave now!

92. OPENING LINE: Stop looking at me!

CLOSING LINE: Sorry. I just can't help myself.

93. OPENING LINE: What in the world happened to you?

CLOSING LINE: I think maybe I'd better get to a hospital.

94. OPENING LINE: Why are you home so early?

CLOSING LINE: Don't worry. I'll find another job.

95. OPENING LINE: I told you yesterday that I never want to see you again!

CLOSING LINE: Maybe someday you will understand.

96. OPENING LINE: Start whenever you're ready.

CLOSING LINE: It's no use. I'm never going to finish this.

97. OPENING LINE: I don't care if you don't believe me. I'm telling the truth!

CLOSING LINE: You're a terrible liar.

98. OPENING LINE: What's the rush? Stay for a while!

CLOSING LINE: I'm glad I stayed.

99. OPENING LINE: It's not whether you win or lose; it's how you play the game.

CLOSING LINE: I'm tired of losing all the time.

100. OPENING LINE: I've been thinking about you all day.

CLOSING LINE: Thank you.

CHANGING LOCATIONS

Picture yourself standing in the middle of a crowded amusement park. Imagine the sights, the smells, the sounds, your feeling of exhilaration as you decide whether to take another ride on the roller coaster or meet your friends at the video arcade. Now imagine yourself sitting in a quiet library, so quiet that you can hear yourself breathe. Around you, others are in deep concentration or browsing through huge stacks of books. Suddenly, you break the silence with a loud sneeze and become embarrassed by the stares from those surrounding you.

Often when our surroundings change, so do our attitudes and feelings. Leaving the comfort of a home for a dentist appointment will certainly result in a mood shift for most people. Listed below are one hundred pairs of acting environments. Direct any number of players to take the stage or playing area, announce the two settings, and then tell them to improvise a scene that takes place in the first location and ends in the second. The players must come up with a reason to leave one place and go to the other. As soon as you give the signal to begin, the players are free to say and do anything they like, as long as what they say and do make sense within the two environments.

Two approaches may be taken when presenting these improvisations. The players may break the scene at the point when they're leaving the first location and then resume the action as they're entering the second, or they may include the action of traveling from one place to the other in the scene.

It might also be fun to have the players improvise the scene twice, with the beginning and ending locations reversed the second time. The second scene could be completely different from the first!

You may use the following questions to guide your discussion of the performances with your players and audience:

- How did the players use the two settings to develop the scene?
- How did the players' attitudes, moods, feelings, and expressions, change as they left the first location and entered the second?
- What conflicts developed as a direct result of the changing settings?
- What did the players see, hear, touch, taste, or smell in each of the two places? Which of their senses played significant roles in the improvisation?
- Do you think that you would have behaved the same way in each setting? If not, what might you have done differently?

1. **FIRST LOCATION:** a nightclub
   SECOND LOCATION: an all-night diner

2. **FIRST LOCATION:** the basement of a five-story apartment building
   SECOND LOCATION: the rooftop of the same building

3. **FIRST LOCATION:** a high school gymnasium
   SECOND LOCATION: a high school principal's office

4. **FIRST LOCATION:** a shopping mall
   SECOND LOCATION: a public swimming pool

5. **FIRST LOCATION:** a modern-art museum
   SECOND LOCATION: a rock concert

6. **FIRST LOCATION:** a restaurant
   SECOND LOCATION: a subway station

7. **FIRST LOCATION:** a private yacht
   SECOND LOCATION: a children's playground

8. FIRST LOCATION: a singles' bar
SECOND LOCATION: a psychiatrist's office

9. FIRST LOCATION: an animal shelter
SECOND LOCATION: a jail cell

10. FIRST LOCATION: a bank building
SECOND LOCATION: an unemployment office

11. FIRST LOCATION: a fire station
SECOND LOCATION: a Laundromat

12. FIRST LOCATION: a supermarket
SECOND LOCATION: a post office

13. FIRST LOCATION: a movie theater
SECOND LOCATION: a drugstore

14. FIRST LOCATION: a hotel lobby
SECOND LOCATION: an empty parking lot

15. FIRST LOCATION: a casino
SECOND LOCATION: a golf course

16. FIRST LOCATION: a flower shop
SECOND LOCATION: a church

17. FIRST LOCATION: a zoo
SECOND LOCATION: a bakery

18. FIRST LOCATION: a junkyard
SECOND LOCATION: an antique store

19. FIRST LOCATION: a toy store
SECOND LOCATION: a rose garden

20. FIRST LOCATION: a street corner
SECOND LOCATION: a hilltop

21. FIRST LOCATION: an island beach
SECOND LOCATION: a rowboat

22. FIRST LOCATION: an airport
SECOND LOCATION: a bookshop

23. FIRST LOCATION: a football field
SECOND LOCATION: a cemetery

24. FIRST LOCATION: a barnyard
SECOND LOCATION: a train station

25. FIRST LOCATION: a bowling alley
SECOND LOCATION: a hospital emergency room

26. FIRST LOCATION: a new-car dealership
SECOND LOCATION: a used-car dealership

27. FIRST LOCATION: an airplane
SECOND LOCATION: an open field

28. FIRST LOCATION: a spaceship
SECOND LOCATION: an ocean bay

29. FIRST LOCATION: a coffee shop
SECOND LOCATION: a dry cleaner

30. FIRST LOCATION: a child care center
SECOND LOCATION: a candy store

31. FIRST LOCATION: a maternity shop
SECOND LOCATION: a courthouse

32. FIRST LOCATION: a trailer park
SECOND LOCATION: a garbage dump

33. FIRST LOCATION: a parking garage
SECOND LOCATION: a library

34. FIRST LOCATION: a health club
SECOND LOCATION: a fast-food restaurant

35. FIRST LOCATION: a pig farm
   SECOND LOCATION: a pet store

36. FIRST LOCATION: a bridal shop
   SECOND LOCATION: a pizzeria

37. FIRST LOCATION: a card store
   SECOND LOCATION: a funeral home

38. FIRST LOCATION: a park
   SECOND LOCATION: a suburban road

39. FIRST LOCATION: a travel agency
   SECOND LOCATION: a Spanish castle

40. FIRST LOCATION: a car on a Ferris wheel
   SECOND LOCATION: a public restroom

41. FIRST LOCATION: a city street
   SECOND LOCATION: a television news studio

42. FIRST LOCATION: a bus stop
   SECOND LOCATION: the front porch of a home

43. FIRST LOCATION: a cruise ship
   SECOND LOCATION: a lifeboat

44. FIRST LOCATION: a winery
   SECOND LOCATION: a brewery

45. FIRST LOCATION: a foxhole
   SECOND LOCATION: a battlefield

46. FIRST LOCATION: a motorboat
   SECOND LOCATION: a small pier

47. FIRST LOCATION: a classroom
   SECOND LOCATION: a cafeteria

48. FIRST LOCATION: an office
   SECOND LOCATION: an elevator

49. FIRST LOCATION: a bookstore
   SECOND LOCATION: a pastry shop

50. FIRST LOCATION: a hardware store
   SECOND LOCATION: a construction site

51. FIRST LOCATION: a rooftop of a tall building
   SECOND LOCATION: a stairwell

52. FIRST LOCATION: a shoe store
   SECOND LOCATION: a formal catering hall

53. FIRST LOCATION: a walk-in closet
   SECOND LOCATION: a department store

54. FIRST LOCATION: a dance club
   SECOND LOCATION: a yoga class

55. FIRST LOCATION: a dark alleyway
   SECOND LOCATION: a storefront

56. FIRST LOCATION: a ski slope
   SECOND LOCATION: a ski lodge

57. FIRST LOCATION: a pup tent
   SECOND LOCATION: a hotel room

58. FIRST LOCATION: a sauna
   SECOND LOCATION: a walk-in refrigerator

59. FIRST LOCATION: a basketball court
   SECOND LOCATION: a locker room

60. FIRST LOCATION: a tree house
   SECOND LOCATION: a home kitchen

61. FIRST LOCATION: a carnival midway
   SECOND LOCATION: a fun house

62. FIRST LOCATION: a haunted house
   SECOND LOCATION: a dark street

63. FIRST LOCATION: a scientific laboratory
   SECOND LOCATION: a morgue

64. FIRST LOCATION: a prison yard
   SECOND LOCATION: an underground tunnel

65. FIRST LOCATION: a mountaintop
   SECOND LOCATION: a cave

66. FIRST LOCATION: a doctor's waiting room
   SECOND LOCATION: a doctor's examination room

67. FIRST LOCATION: a stage in a theater
   SECOND LOCATION: the lobby of a theater

68. FIRST LOCATION: an animal shelter
   SECOND LOCATION: a veterinary clinic

69. FIRST LOCATION: a dressing room in a clothing store
   SECOND LOCATION: a cocktail bar

70. FIRST LOCATION: an optometrist's examination room
   SECOND LOCATION: a pistol range

71. FIRST LOCATION: the kitchen of a restaurant
   SECOND LOCATION: a garbage truck

72. FIRST LOCATION: a music store
   SECOND LOCATION: a recording studio

73. FIRST LOCATION: a mausoleum
   SECOND LOCATION: a comedy club

74. FIRST LOCATION: an aviary
   SECOND LOCATION: an aquarium

75. FIRST LOCATION: the edge of a cliff
   SECOND LOCATION: a ravine

76. FIRST LOCATION: an automated car wash
   SECOND LOCATION: a driveway

77. FIRST LOCATION: a circus tent
   SECOND LOCATION: a concession stand

78. FIRST LOCATION: a food court in a mall
   SECOND LOCATION: an escalator

79. FIRST LOCATION: a country road
   SECOND LOCATION: a corn field

80. FIRST LOCATION: a four-lane highway
   SECOND LOCATION: a narrow bridge

81. FIRST LOCATION: a costume shop
   SECOND LOCATION: a jewelry store

82. FIRST LOCATION: a baseball field
   SECOND LOCATION: a dugout

83. FIRST LOCATION: a cranberry bog
   SECOND LOCATION: a grocery store

84. FIRST LOCATION: an ice-skating rink
   SECOND LOCATION: a roller-skating rink

85. FIRST LOCATION: a corn maze
   SECOND LOCATION: a grain silo

86. FIRST LOCATION: a garden center
   SECOND LOCATION: the backyard of a home

87. FIRST LOCATION: an airport runway
   SECOND LOCATION: an airport traffic control tower

88. FIRST LOCATION: a tanning salon
SECOND LOCATION: an employment agency

89. FIRST LOCATION: a bicycle path
SECOND LOCATION: a sidewalk

90. FIRST LOCATION: a boxing ring
SECOND LOCATION: a hospital operating room

91. FIRST LOCATION: a walk-in safe
SECOND LOCATION: a bank manager's office

92. FIRST LOCATION: a duck pond
SECOND LOCATION: an animal hospital

93. FIRST LOCATION: a tour bus
SECOND LOCATION: a recital hall

94. FIRST LOCATION: a nail salon
SECOND LOCATION: a hair salon

95. FIRST LOCATION: an outdoor basketball court
SECOND LOCATION: a lemonade stand

96. FIRST LOCATION: a college dormitory
SECOND LOCATION: a college lecture hall

97. FIRST LOCATION: a desert oasis
SECOND LOCATION: a desert beach

98. FIRST LOCATION: a psychiatric ward
SECOND LOCATION: a police station

99. FIRST LOCATION: a snow-covered field
SECOND LOCATION: a warm house

100. FIRST LOCATION: a mansion
SECOND LOCATION: a small shack

USING PROPS

If you're in a familiar place right now, stop and look around you. You're probably surrounded by things you've seen a thousand times before. Perhaps some belong to you, or maybe they belong to people you know. Most likely, many of these objects bring to mind particular memories, and some might even elicit an emotional response.

Just as objects can trigger specific thoughts, props can trigger an actor's creativity. Let's say you're given a pencil and then asked to improvise a scene in which it plays a major part. What might you do with a pencil? Your most obvious choice is to write with it. You might write a letter or a grocery list. If you're a bit more creative, you might use the pencil for something other than writing or drawing. You might pry open a lid or maybe punch holes in the top of a shoebox. You're only limited by your imagination.

On the following pages is a list of groups of three common objects. To run the improvisations, select two or three players, assign them three props to be used in the scene, and have them take the stage. Don't suggest role relationships, conflicts, obstacles, or any kind of setting. Their characters and actions should simply evolve from the function and use of the props. Each item must play a key role in the scene. This will be challenging since the items in each group purposely have no obvious connection to each other. At the end of the improvisation, the audience should be able to easily identify which three items were central to the scene.

These scenes may be performed with or without the actual props. If the props are not available, the players can simply pantomime the use of them. As a fun alternative, if you have the actual props available, tell the players to use the prop for something other than its intended purpose. This will force the actor to stretch his imagination even further. For example, a pencil might be used as a conductor's baton, a knitting needle, a dart, or anything else its shape and size might suggest.

Use the following questions to guide your discussion of the improvisations:

- Were you able to easily identify which three objects were central to the scene?
- Was each prop truly a key element of the improvisation?
- Did the players make creative use of their props?
- Would you have used the props differently?

1. shoe, book, dinner plate

2. broom, can opener, toilet paper roll

3. feather duster, potted plant, clock

4. gravy boat, dental floss, golf ball

5. pillowcase, stapler, wire hanger

6. car keys, buttons, rubber band

7. pencil sharpener, ashtray, string

8. toothbrush, ice bucket, mousetrap

9. coasters, lightbulb, curtain rod

10. thumbtacks, washcloth, thermometer

11. rolling pin, notebook, nail clippers

12. dog collar, paper clips, cocktail shaker

13. wallet, vase, hammer

14. alarm clock, toilet brush, cookie sheets

15. watering can, tea bags, television remote control

16. bar of soap, banana, wristwatch

17. balloon, salt shaker, candlestick

18. coffee cup, cuff links, pair of dice

19. potato peeler, stopwatch, mittens

20. dog collar, safety pins, baseball cap

21. plastic flowers, sombrero, mobile phone

22. fortune cookies, marbles, envelopes

23. newspaper, plunger, plastic cups

24. adhesive bandage, can of spray paint, empty beer mug

25. baby bottle, AAA batteries, fire extinguisher

26. sponge, spoon, bracelet

27. wrench, purse, plastic bags

28. dartboard, picture frame, flashlight

29. flyswatter, refrigerator magnet, clothespin

30. scissors, hot dog buns, hair curlers

31. microphone, matchbox, plastic sand shovel

32. compact mirror, tree branch, guitar string

33. bath towel, earrings, blender

34. laundry bag, fishhooks, mothballs

35. can of hairspray, paper coffee filters, slippers

36. power strip, bicycle chain, vinyl gloves

37. hair clip, calculator, screwdriver

38. 2-pound barbell, stuffed animal, spice rack

39. jewelry box, measuring tape, steel wool pad

40. concert tickets, thimble, feathers

41. camera, cat toys, empty cereal box

42. house key, sheet of waxed paper, masking tape

43. bottle cap, roller skates, bedsheets

44. shoelaces, harmonica, bottle of sunscreen

45. cigar, threading needle, wall calendar

46. oven mitt, golf tee, fishing pole

47. sunglasses, pocket comb, seashells

48. umbrella, thimble, paper fan

49. candy bar, folding chair, beach ball

50. sweater, ice cube tray, dog biscuit

51. snow boots, hairnet, surgical mask

52. snorkel, binoculars, tissue box

53. postage stamps, straight pins, wooden ruler

54. reading glasses, compass, glue stick

55. magnifying glass, belt, water bottle

56. bicycle bell, toothpicks, sugar cubes

57. ping-pong paddle, rubber ducky, cough drops

58. test tube, globe, horseshoes

59. bowling ball, drinking glass, desk lamp

60. popsicle stick, tennis racquet, earmuffs

61. headphones, paper airplane, CD

62. poker chips, wire cutters, sweatshirt

63. frying pan, billiard balls, shot glass

64. garden hose, ball of yarn, microscope

65. protractor, hourglass, adhesive tape

66. roll of duct tape, toy boat, coloring book

67. candelabra, golf club, tuning fork

68. stepladder, handkerchief, deck of playing cards

69. coffee beans, personal fan, pliers

70. boxing gloves, knitting needles, wastepaper basket

71. bow tie, notepad, wine bottle cork

72. bricks, birdhouse, hand sanitizer

73. paper napkin, pencil case, hockey mask

74. bridal veil, birthday candles, pack of chewing gum

75. ice pick, corkscrew, teddy bear

76. bottle of dishwashing liquid, prism, guitar pick

77. paper bag, doorknob, dog leash

78. empty pill bottle, plastic knife, jump rope

79. baby shoes, bottle of cologne, wine glass

80. screws, bathroom scale, nose hair trimmer

81. stethoscope, hair ribbon, laptop

82. headband, potato masher, earplugs

83. measuring cup, party horn, eye patch

84. jar lid, cardboard box, grass clippings

85. birthday card, cotton balls, tweezers

86. ink pad, wrapping paper, nail polish

87. credit cards, fireplace poker, peanut shells

88. candy wrappers, water pistol, shaving cream

89. garbage bags, eyedropper, curling iron

90. waffle iron, can of motor oil, dustpan

91. drain cleaner, jigsaw puzzle, shopping basket

92. vacuum cleaner, roasting pan, diary

93. deodorant spray, fish tank, ballpoint pen

94. suitcase, lampshade, spinning top

95. party hat, dish towel, drinking straw

96. tea strainer, jellybeans, wig

97. spatula, music box, nutcracker

98. slotted spoon, cigar case, peach pits

99. birdfeeder, candy cane, modeling clay

100. dollar bill, salad dressing, basketball

UNREAL IMPROVISATIONS

It's not uncommon to personify inanimate objects in everyday conversation: The wind is howling. That cake is calling my name. The words leaped off the paper. The fire ran wild. Life is passing me by.

It's also not uncommon for us to speak to nonhuman things as if they were human. Have you ever screamed at your computer for crashing while you were writing an important e-mail? You may have begged your car to start on a cold morning. You've probably told your alarm clock to shut up more than once in your life.

It's fun to think of what things would say if they could talk. Imagine a dress saying, "I wish she'd stop asking her husband if I make her look fat! It is not my intention to make anyone look fat!" But what would its voice sound like? How would it posture itself if it could stand? If it could walk, what kind of a stride might it have?

Improvising objects and animals allows actors a chance to move, gesture, and vocalize in ways that can be completely outside the realm of human nature. Physicalizing the imagined thoughts and emotions of inanimate objects and animals is an excellent way for actors to completely step outside of themselves and avoid stereotypical visible and vocal expressions.

Running the improvisations in this chapter is simple. Just ask the players to take the stage or acting area, read the scene summary aloud, and let the players take it from there. You can give the players a time limit or allow them to end the scene on their own. After the performance is over, you might want to discuss with the players and the observers the characteristics of the objects or animals used to develop specific feelings, actions, and objectives.

Note: A few simple facts about the animals in the "Living Things" section are included to make it easier for the players to develop their characters. If needed, allow the players a few minutes before performing to find more detailed information.

Inanimate Objects

Two Players

1. A smartphone brags about its fancy features to a simple landline phone.

2. A dime reminds a nickel that the value of a coin has little to do with its size.

3. A permanent marker accuses a pencil of being fickle, since anything written in pencil can be easily erased.

4. An expensive oil painting isn't happy with the simple wooden frame that surrounds it.

5. As dinnertime draws near, a knife and a fork develop a plan of attack.

6. A polka-dotted dress shirt and a striped tie are attracted to each other, even though they realize they don't match.

7. Bruised and battered, a baseball begs a baseball bat not to swing at it.

8. Two peas in a pod swear they'll always be together.

9. A loveseat becomes romantically involved with a large sofa.

10. A 12-foot extension ladder bullies a small stepstool.

11. A roll of dental floss and a toothbrush debate their individual importance in the war on tooth decay.

12. Lamenting the popularity of tablets and electronic reading devices, two books reminisce about the old days.

13. An energy-efficient LED light bulb criticizes an incandescent light bulb for its inefficient and wasteful lifestyle.

14. An acoustic guitar mocks a ukulele for its small size and high-pitched tone.

15. A pair of sunglasses tries to convince a pair of reading glasses to go outside into the bright sunshine with him.

16. A hammer apologizes to a nail before hitting it on the head.

17. A ball of string promises a kite that it will stay strong, no matter how windy it becomes.

18. A snow shovel solicits the help of a large, high-powered snow blower.

19. Feeling overworked, a kitchen sink is happy to meet a newly installed dishwasher.

20. A roller skate and an ice skate discuss their similarities and differences.

21. An abacus is amazed by the speed and accuracy of a calculator.

22. A laptop shares its stories on the road with a jealous desktop computer.

23. A wall clock asks a wristwatch what it's like to keep time while wrapped around a person's wrist.

24. Having endured a daily onslaught of hot oil and greasy foods, a frying pan seeks the council of a deep fryer, who inarguably has a much more difficult life.

25. A stopwatch listens with great interest to a sand timer's stories about its rich ancestry.

26. A corkscrew is confused when it meets a bottle of wine with a screw cap.

27. A hairbrush needs a comb's help to create a perfect hairstyle.

28. Tired of living in a small, cramped cardboard box, a cigarette asks a cigar if he can move into its spacious, comfortable humidor with it.

29. An apple challenges an orange's contention that the orange is the most popular fruit in the supermarket's produce section.

30. A clothes dryer tries to comfort a broken washing machine just before a repairman is scheduled to arrive.

31. A flat-heeled shoe accuses a high-heeled shoe of being pretentious.

32. An angry steel ball wants a persistent magnet to leave him alone.

33. Two kernels of popcorn anticipate the day they will be reborn as fully popped popcorn.

34. A dart warns a dartboard that it will soon make its way toward the board's bull's-eye and gouge him.

35. A lampshade tells a lightbulb that it's too bright for its own good.

36. An electric razor wishes to know why a single razor blade has such hatred for it.

37. A match helps an unlit candle realize its full potential.

38. The Earth praises the Sun for its life-supporting light and warmth.

39. Discouraged by its low position, an ankle bracelet asks a wrist bracelet if it wouldn't mind trading places every once in a while.

40. A regular slice of pizza advises a slice of "everything" pizza to simplify its life.

41. A recycling bin encourages a plastic bottle to jump inside of it and begin a new life.

42. A cellphone case promises a cellphone to do its best to protect it.

43. A hamburger takes issue with a french fry's claim that a burger would be nothing without a side of fries.

44. A CD is bewildered when a vinyl record explains that it's making a comeback.

45. A large SUV ridicules a compact car's size and lack of power.

46. A pencil thanks a pencil sharpener for giving it a shave.

47. Two ice cubes begin to panic when their freezer's power source is disconnected.

48. A doormat cautions a muddy shoe to stay away from it.

49. The ace of spades in a deck of cards is not amused by the deck's joker.

50. A digital SLR camera suggests that a smartphone should stick to phone calls and text messages and stop doing what cameras can do better.

51. A blade of grass urges a dandelion to leave before it gets sprayed with weed killer.

52. A snow boot and a work boot disagree over which of them has a tougher life.

53. A roll of painter's tape becomes jealous when a roll of duct tape tells it about the hundreds of ways duct tape can be used.

54. A large padded envelope tells a single, first-class postage stamp that it will need to bring along a few more of its friends if it wants to travel through the mail with it.

55. A toaster oven advises a microwave to slow down and enjoy life.

56. A reusable canvas grocery bag scolds a plastic bag for being environmentally unfriendly.

57. A martini glass filled with gin invites an olive to jump in.

58. A deflated tire is happy to meet an air pump.

59. An oil can intends to silence a squeaky wheel.

60. An old standard-definition television is tired of listening to a young, high-definition television brag about how sharp it is.

61. A pillow asks to be set free from its pillowcase.

62. A knife sharpener agrees to give an old, dull knife a complete makeover.

63. A travel mug entertains a simple coffee cup with its stories of the road.

64. A racing bicycle tells a bicycle with training wheels not to be anxious to grow up too fast.

65. A slotted spoon explains its purpose and use to a curious soup ladle.

66. A cocktail napkin reprimands a cold beer bottle for standing directly on an unprotected wooden bar.

67. Tired of being dribbled on, a saucer asks its partner cup to be a little less messy.

68. A nail clipper and a nail file are excited to be working in a new nail salon.

69. A piece of copper pipe expresses his nervousness as a welding torch approaches it.

70. A piece of sandpaper tries to smooth things over with a block of wood.

71. A wallet admires a purse for its ability to hold so many things.

72. A fishnet assures a fishhook that it will be ready to secure the catch of the day when the time arrives.

73. A balloon warns a straight pin to keep its distance.

74. A salt shaker and a pepper shaker become dizzy after seasoning a large steak.

75. A lighter is anxious to set off a firecracker.

Three Players

76. A basketball and a soccer ball tease a football about its odd shape.

77. Unsure of the best way to connect itself with others of its kind, a sheet of paper seeks advice from a stapler and a paper clip.

78. Two fearless bowling pins positioned on opposite sides of the lane dare a bowling ball to knock both of them down in a single try.

79. A snobby champagne glass is not enjoying the company of a vivacious beer mug and a spirited shot glass.

80. A zipper informs a couple of buttons that it will soon replace them on a winter coat.

81. A maxi skirt berates a miniskirt and a pair of micro shorts for being too flirtatious.

82. An Olympic silver medal and an Olympic bronze medal are miffed by an Olympic gold medal's swagger.

83. A tissue, a paper napkin, and a paper towel argue over which of them has the worst job.

84. A forlorn yellow plastic cup and a depressed blue plastic cup ask a cheerful red plastic cup why red cups are the most popular choices at parties.

85. An elliptical machine and a treadmill welcome a new stationary bicycle to the gym.

86. Knowing it will soon be picked and shipped to a floral shop, a red rose resting on its vine bids farewell to its orchid and daisy garden friends on the day before Valentine's Day.

87. A drill, a screwdriver, and a wrench mentally prepare themselves for another day on the workbench.

88. A key ring attempts to settle an argument between a house key and car key that always seem to be colliding.

89. A clock's hour, minute, and second hands become bored keeping time.

90. Two matching socks help a single sock find its lost partner.

91. Three coins in a fountain argue over which will provide the most luck for the person who tossed them in.

92. A suit jacket, vest, and trousers discuss their plans for a night out on the town.

93. The three flavors in a carton of Neapolitan ice cream—vanilla, chocolate, and strawberry—debate which of the three is considered a favorite by most.

94. Since it only makes short appearances, the yellow light in a traffic light tells the red and green lights that it would like equal billing with them.

95. Frankincense, gold, and myrrh get ready for the first Christmas.

96. A paper, rock, and scissors play a competitive game together.

97. A knife and a fork accuse a spoon of not working as hard as they do during dinner.

98. The sun, the moon, and a star contemplate their role in the universe.

99. A computer's Escape key shares its plan to break away from the keyboard with the Shift and Tab key.

100. A saxophone and a trumpet tease a piccolo about its small size.

Animals

....

Two Players

1. A deer and an antelope play together on their home on the range.
FACT: The classic song "Home on the Range" includes the lyric "Home, home on the range / Where the deer and the antelope play."

2. A trout tries to convince a salmon that it would be easier to swim downstream than upstream.
FACT: Salmon swim upstream to lay and fertilize their eggs.

3. An anteater spots an appetizing termite emerging from its mound.
FACT: Anteaters prey on termites and other insects.

4. A bald eagle explains to a condor why the eagle is America's national bird, even though an eagle is a bit smaller than a condor.
FACT: The condor's wingspan is among the largest of all birds.

5. A mouse dares a cat to try to catch it.
FACT: Mice can squeeze through small gaps and use their strong teeth to bite through obstacles.

6. Proud of its speed, a cheetah challenges a greyhound to a race.
FACT: The greyhound is one of the fastest dog breeds, but the cheetah is the fastest land animal on earth.

7. A young sparrow asks an owl for life advice.
FACT: "Wise as an owl" is a common folk expression.

8. A gray fox outfoxes a red fox.
FACT: "Sly as a fox" is a common saying.

9. A common tree squirrel asks a flying squirrel how it learned to fly.

> **FACT:** Flying squirrels don't actually fly; they glide from tree to tree by extending the membranes that stretch between their front and hind legs.

10. An unintelligible giraffe tells a frightened frog that it has a frog in its throat.

> **FACT:** Giraffes are normally very social animals that rarely fight.

11. A honeybee asks a bumblebee to help it get out of a sticky situation.

> **FACT:** Honeybees produce honey.

12. An emu advises an ostrich to get its head out of the sand and face reality.

> **FACT:** The ostrich is the largest bird on earth; the emu is the second largest. Ostriches don't actually bury their heads in the sand when they're frightened. Sometimes they pick at the sand in search of insects, and from a distance it may appear as if they're burying their heads in the sand.

13. A squid tries to avoid being spotted by a hungry tiger shark.

> **FACT:** The squid is a main prey of the tiger shark.

14. A kangaroo challenges a jackrabbit to a hopping contest.

> **FACT:** Both kangaroos and jackrabbits can hop at speeds up to forty miles per hour.

15. A crab asks a barnacle if it plans to stick around.

> **FACT:** Soon after birth, barnacles attach themselves to rocks and other solid objects and remain there for the duration of their lives.

16. During early morning, a bird tries to catch a worm.

> **FACT:** "The early bird catches the worm" is a proverb meaning that starting to work on something immediately will result in success.

17. A nightingale and a mockingbird sing together.

> **FACT:** The nightingale and the mockingbird are both known for singing loudly and beautifully.

18. Walking together, a sloth tries to keep up with a bunny rabbit.

> **FACT:** A rabbit can leap as far as three yards at a time.

19. A dolphin attempts to persuade a killer whale to look elsewhere for a meal.

> **FACT:** The dolphin is considered to be one of the world's most intelligent animals. Killer whales often prey on dolphins.

20. A wolverine warns a moose not to be deceived by its small size.

> **FACT:** A wolverine is capable of hunting down and killing animals much larger than itself.

21. A dingo asks a Labrador retriever what it's like to live in a house with humans.

> **FACT:** Dingoes live in the wild but were once thought to be domesticated dogs.

22. A friendly walrus befriends a tired seabird.

> **FACT:** Seabirds migrate extremely long distances.

23. A hawk swoops down from the sky to attack a koala bear but doesn't have the heart to harm the cute animal.

> **FACT:** Hawks have been known to prey on koala bears, which many consider to be among the most adorable animals in the world.

24. A guinea pig's loud squealing annoys a hamster.

> **FACT:** Guinea pigs communicate with high-pitched squeals.

25. A small lizard is impressed by the size and rarity of a Komodo dragon.

> **FACT:** The Komodo dragon is the largest and arguably the most powerful lizard in existence. It can only be found on five Indonesian islands and is in danger of extinction.

26. An Irish setter and an Italian greyhound chat about their ancestry.

FACT: The Irish setter and the Italian greyhound are both large dogs.

27. A Great Dane and a Chihuahua discuss the advantages and disadvantages of their individual sizes.

FACT: Small dogs tend to live longer than large dogs. The average life span of a Great Dane is six to eight years, one of the shortest for all dog breeds; the average life span of a Chihuahua is ten to eighteen years, one of the longest for all dog breeds.

28. An angelfish insists that its clownfish friend take life more seriously.

FACT: The orange and white patterned colors of a clownfish suggest the appearance of a clown. The angelfish has a triangular shape.

29. A monkey suspects that a little weasel stole its banana.

FACT: Weasels have a reputation for being quick and nimble.

30. A pig resents being called a slob by a fastidious housecat.

FACT: Under the right conditions, the pig is actually a clean animal.

31. A badger wants an armadillo to come out of its shell.

FACT: An armadillo withdraws into its shell when it feels threatened. The badger has a vicious bite.

32. A black widow asserts that it's more dangerous than a scorpion.

FACT: A black widow's venom is highly potent.

33. A butterfly tells a caterpillar that it will one day emerge from a cocoon with wings and become a butterfly.

FACT: Most species of caterpillars live for a few months before entering their cocoons and then usually live for two weeks or less after emerging as butterflies.

34. A newt and a frog share a rock together.

> **FACT:** Newts and frogs spend much of their lives in ponds and streams.

35. A slug admires a snail's shell.

> **FACT:** A slug is essentially a snail without an exterior shell.

36. A great white shark makes fun of a hammerhead shark's flat head.

> **FACT:** The great white shark is generally more aggressive than the hammerhead. The hammerhead shark's flat head enhances its ability to find its prey.

37. An old wasp warns a young wasp not to sting anyone, since wasps often die after they use their stingers.

> **FACT:** Not all wasps can sting, but those that do may die after stinging because the stinger can fall off.

38. A gorilla and a dolphin share an intelligent conversation together.

> **FACT:** Gorillas and dolphins are considered to be two of the most intelligent animals in the world.

39. Thinking a cow had been calling, a common toad is surprised when a bullfrog shows up.

> **FACT:** Bullfrogs produce a call that sounds similar to a cow mooing loudly.

40. An oyster joins a clam for drinks at a clam bar.

> **FACT:** Oysters produce valuable pearls; clams do not produce pearls.

41. An Antarctic penguin visits an African penguin and complains about the heat.

> **FACT:** Most people associate penguins with the South Pole, but some species, such as the African penguin, thrive in warm climates.

42. A desert tortoise emerges from its underground hiding space and meets a camel, and the two take a slow walk through the desert, contemplating life in a dry, hot climate.

> **FACT:** The desert tortoise and the camel are both slow-moving animals.

43. A badger takes a swimming lesson from an otter.

> **FACT:** The badger and the otter are thought to be in the same animal family, but the badger is not an aquatic animal.

44. A beagle admires a standard poodle's fancy grooming.

> **FACT:** The hindquarters and legs of a standard poodle are traditionally shaved, and rounded puffs of fur are left on the hips, tail, and ankles.

45. A ladybug tells a housefly to buzz off.

> **FACT:** Ladybugs don't make a buzzing sound.

46. A seahorse refuses to give a tired guppy a ride on its back.

> **FACT:** The seahorse's snout gives it an appearance similar to a horse.

47. An alligator and a crocodile argue over which is better looking.

> **FACT:** Alligators are usually smaller than crocodiles and have U-shaped snouts. Crocodiles have V-shaped snouts.

48. A Siamese fighting fish picks a fight with a neon tetra.

> **FACT:** The Siamese fighting fish will behave aggressively toward any smaller fish it sees as a threat.

49. A duck is jealous of all the attention a swan is getting.

> **FACT:** Swans have gray or brown feathers until they're about two years old. Adult swans have pure-white feathers and long, graceful necks.

50. A pheasant tells a male peacock to stop showing off all its fancy tail feathers.

> **FACT:** The pheasant and the peacock are related. The pheasant has brightly colored feathers, but the male peacock's intricate display of large, colorful tail feathers is unique among all birds.

51. A chicken and a turkey exchange strategies on how to avoid becoming someone's dinner.

> **FACT:** Chickens and turkeys are very intelligent. Both can vocalize as many as thirty distinct sounds to communicate different meanings.

52. A pelican and a seagull explore the ocean together.

> **FACT:** The pelican and the seagull are both water birds. The pelican has a pouch in its throat that it uses to catch fish.

53. A river turtle asks a tortoise to reveal its secret to a long life.

> **FACT:** The river turtle's lifespan is about thirty years; the tortoise's lifespan is one hundred years, and some have been known to live more than 150 years.

54. A doubtful robin listens to a kiwi explain that it's actually a bird.

> **FACT:** The kiwi is a bird, but it can't fly.

55. A leopard seal advises a curious barracuda to keep moving.

> **FACT:** The leopard seal is an aggressive animal that doesn't have many natural predators.

56. A bull shark invites a stingray over for dinner.

> **FACT:** The bull shark is one of the most dangerous species of sharks and often preys on stingrays.

57. A goose tries to avoid conversing with a loon.

> **FACT:** A loon is a water bird similar to a duck, but it's also an informal term for a foolish person.

58. Having just read "The Rime of the Ancient Mariner," a tropicbird is excited to meet an albatross.

> **FACT:** The albatross is featured in Samuel Taylor Coleridge's famous poem "The Rime of the Ancient Mariner." Because of the poem, the albatross has become symbolic of a burden or curse placed on someone.

59. A large bison intimidates a cow.

> **FACT:** The bison is a type of cow and is thought to be the largest land animal living in North America.

60. Unable to sleep, a squirrel monkey begs a howler monkey to keep it down.

> **FACT:** The squirrel monkey is a small species of monkey. The howler monkey is one of the largest species and has a howling voice that can be heard for miles.

61. A mouse tries to convince a hungry rattlesnake that there are other rodents in the area much tastier than mice.

> **FACT:** Rattlesnakes prey on mice.

62. A tree frog angrily asks a woodpecker to stop pecking on its tree.

> **FACT:** A woodpecker drills into trees with its beak to dig out insects under the bark. It can peck at a rate of up to twenty pecks per second!

63. A hedgehog tells a porcupine that it's looking sharp today.

> **FACT:** Porcupines have long, sharp quills that protect them from predators. Hedgehogs also have quills, but they're much shorter and softer than a porcupine's.

64. An earthworm on a fishhook explains to a fish the consequences of eating it.

> **FACT:** Earthworms help improve the water-holding ability of garden soil.

65. A platypus helps a busy beaver find sticks and twigs for its dam.

   FACT: Beavers build sturdy dams with sticks and twigs. A platypus has a beaver-like tail and spends most of its time in the water.

66. An ant asks an earwig if there's any truth to the rumor that it likes to crawl inside human ears and lay its eggs there.

   FACT: Earwigs live under rocks and logs and often hide in narrow cracks and crevices during the daylight hours. Their name derives from the myth that they crawl inside people's ears when they're sleeping and lay eggs in their brains. There are no scientific facts to support this.

67. Thinking they might be related, a heron inquires about a stork's family background.

   FACT: Herons and cranes are similar in appearance but are not related. Also, a heron flies with its neck retracted, unlike the stork, which flies with its neck outstretched.

68. A young robin admires its father's orange breast.

   FACT: A robin's breast doesn't turn orange until about eight weeks after developing its wing feathers.

69. A grizzly bear dares a black bear to climb down from a tree and face him.

   FACT: Grizzly bears are dangerously aggressive and have few animal predators. Black bears are usually tranquil unless threatened.

70. A white-tailed deer asks a reindeer if there's any truth to the rumor that it can fly.

   FACT: Reindeer fly in Clement Clarke Moore's famous poem "A Visit From St. Nicholas" (also known as "The Night Before Christmas").

71. Considering it a dirty creature, a beetle refuses to associate with a cockroach.

> **FACT:** Cockroaches are often found in garbage pails feeding off food scraps and are therefore considered by many to be disgusting, filthy creatures. Some cockroaches are actually good for the environment because they ingest and recycle organic decomposing material.

72. A catfish finds an electric eel's behavior shocking.

> **FACT:** Electric eels can generate strong electric shocks with enough power to harm large animals.

73. A barn owl tells a tawny owl that it doesn't give a hoot about anything.

> **FACT:** Unlike the tawny owl, the barn owl doesn't hoot. Instead, it produces a high-pitched screech.

74. A sunfish is amazed by the size of a blue whale.

> **FACT:** The blue whale is the largest living creature on Earth.

75. A mouse asks a gecko why it's hiding behind a picture frame on a wall.

> **FACT:** Many cultures believe that a gecko inside your house will bring good luck.

Three Players

76. A hyena finds it hysterically funny when a baboon continually asks an unamused gnu, "What's new?"

> **FACT:** The pronunciation of the word *gnu* is similar to the pronunciation of the word *new*. Hyenas are considered to be extremely intelligent animals. They can produce a loud scream that sounds like a human laugh.

77. A female and a male glowworm laugh at another male glowworm that's trying to mate with a streetlight.

> **FACT:** The purpose of a female glowworm's glow is to attract a mate, but some male glowworms are known to have been attracted to man-made light sources.

78. A hippopotamus, an elephant, and a whale are tired of all the fat jokes.

> **FACT:** The hippo, the elephant, and the whale are three of the largest animals on earth.

79. Three Arctic wolves are happy to see the sun.

> **FACT:** Arctic wolves live in the Arctic Circle, where it is dark five months out of the year. They are also capable of coping with sub-zero temperatures.

80. A chameleon asks a sand lizard and a gecko for suggestions on which color it should become for an upcoming reptile party.

> **FACT:** Chameleons can change colors to blend in with their surroundings.

81. A goat and a sheep are becoming bored listening to a yak complain about its life.

> **FACT:** Yaks have been used to pull weighty farm equipment and move heavy loads through mountainous regions. Yak is also a slang term for incessant talking.

82. A burrowing frog attempts to attract the attention of a nearby spider and worm.

> **FACT:** Burrowing frogs catch insects, worms, and other prey with their long, sticky tongues.

83. Three sea lions bask in the sun together.

> **FACT:** Groups of sea lions often congregate in the sun together.

84. A water buffalo invites two irritated African buffalos to relax in the water with him.

> **FACT:** Water buffalos have been domesticated, but African buffalos are fierce and aggressive.

85. A panther asks a leopard and a jaguar where they got their fancy, spotted coats.

> **FACT:** Panthers, leopards, and jaguars are similar in appearance, except that leopards and jaguars have spotted coats and panthers have solid coats. The spots on the coats of a jaguar and a leopard are called rosettes. A jaguar's rosettes include tiny, little spots. A leopard's rosettes are smaller and don't include the small spots.

86. A cardinal becomes annoyed listening to two parrots conversing.

> **FACT:** Parrots mimic human speech in short, repeated words and phrases.

87. Two male tarantulas compete for the attention of a female tarantula.

> **FACT:** The female tarantula is larger and lives longer than the male.

88. A stallion bestows his years of wisdom on a filly and a colt.

> **FACT:** A stallion is an adult male horse, a filly is a young female horse, and a colt is a young male horse.

89. A guinea pig, a gerbil, and a hamster argue over which rodent makes the best house pet.

> **FACT:** Guinea pigs are very sociable and come in a variety of colors. Gerbils are energetic and love using the exercise wheels in their cages. Hamsters are more active at night and love to chew on things.

90. Two lemmings convince a third lemming not to jump off a cliff.

FACT: Lemmings occasionally fall from cliffs when searching for food, but the belief that they commit mass suicide by jumping is a myth.

91. A male and a female mountain lion help their baby navigate the mountainside.

FACT: Mountain lions cannot see clearly until they are about three months old.

92. A baboon and a chimpanzee compliment a mandrill on its colorful nose.

FACT: A mandrill has a blue- and red-colored nose.

93. A friendly pheasant tries to start a conversation with two quails.

FACT: Quails are solitary birds that normally spend their time alone or paired with another quail.

94. Two houseflies gape at a nearby dragonfly.

FACT: Dragonflies are colorful and have wings that sparkle and shine.

95. A border collie tries to inspire a bulldog and a pug to run around and play with him.

FACT: Border collies are extremely energetic. Bulldogs and pugs typically enjoy sleeping.

96. Two young squid ask a fifteen-year-old squid how it managed to live such a long life.

FACT: Most squid are caught and consumed after only a few years, but uncaught squid can live up to fifteen years.

97. Three jackals are worried because they can't find the rest of their pack.

FACT: Jackals normally travel in large packs.

98. A housecat tries to civilize two feral cats.

> **FACT:** Feral cats can thrive in both rural regions and inner cities and tend to be just as healthy as cats that live indoors.

99. Two cows try to convince a bull not to run off and join the rodeo.

> **FACT:** Bulls are strong and aggressive and haven't been castrated, which makes them capable of breeding.

100. A mastiff, a Samoyed, and a rottweiler argue over which of them works the hardest.

> **FACT:** The mastiff, the Samoyed, and the rottweiler are large, working breed dogs.

HISTORICALLY SPEAKING

If Sophocles and Arthur Miller could have collaborated on a play, what kinds of struggles would the protagonist have faced? If Mozart and Jimi Hendrix could have written a song together, what would it have sounded like? If Elizabeth Taylor could have given marriage advice to Anne Boleyn, what suggestions might she have offered?

It's fun to imagine what the most fascinating people from different periods of history might have done together or spoken about if they could have met, especially if they had common interests. Since most popular historical figures had talents and abilities unique for their time, improvising conversations and activities between famous people from different ages is a great way for an actor to explore unusual character complexities.

Of course, it's important for the players to know some facts about the historical figures they will be portraying before starting the improvisation. Have your players do a little bit of research on the people they will be portraying before beginning the scene.

Once they know enough about their characters, simply have two players take the stage or playing area. Read the scene summary aloud to both the players and the audience, and then signal the players to begin. You may impose a time limit on the scene or just allow the players to conclude the scene on their own.

All scenes should take place during the present time and in a non–specific location, rather than during the time period or setting of one of the historical figures. Also, there's no need to rationalize how or why they were brought together.

After each improvisation, you may wish to discuss the following with your players and the audience:

- Did any specific conflicts develop during the scene? If so, how were they resolved?
- Did the historical figures speak and behave as you imagined?
- Were any of the historical figures represented in a stereotypical fashion?
- Did you learn anything new about the characters?

1. Marilyn Monroe (1926–1962) sings "Happy Birthday" to Abraham Lincoln (1809–1865) on his birthday.

2. Leonardo da Vinci (1452–1519) critiques Andy Warhol's (1928–1987) artwork.

3. Harriet Tubman (1822–1913) and Malcolm X (1925–1965) discuss their views on human rights in America.

4. Queen Elizabeth I (1533–1603) explains to Catherine the Great (1729–1796) why she never married.

5. Confucius (551–479 B.C.) and Karl Marx (1818–1883) share their thoughts on religion, politics, and society.

6. Marie Antoinette (1755–1793) offers Princess Diana (1961–1997) advice on handling the press.

7. Mahatma Gandhi (1869–1948) and Martin Luther King, Jr. (1929–1968) exchange ideas on social justice and the importance of nonviolent protest.

8. Maya Angelou (1928–2014) and Emily Dickinson (1830–1886) write a poem together.

9. Ludwig van Beethoven (1770–1827) gives a piano lesson to Liberace (1919–1987).

10. George Washington (1732–1799) thanks Christopher Columbus (1451–1506) for discovering America.

11. Galileo (1564–1642) asks Neil Armstrong (1930–2012) about his trip to the moon.

12. Martha Washington (1731–1802) and Mary Todd Lincoln (1818–1882) discuss the challenges they faced as wives of popular presidents.

13. Pocahontas (1595–1617) inspires Walt Disney (1901–1966) with her life story.

14. Susan B. Anthony (1820–1906) and Eva Perón (1919–1952) compare their personal struggles.

15. Copernicus (1473–1543) and Charles Darwin (1809–1882) recall their dealings with skeptics and disbelievers.

16. Amelia Earhart (1897–1937) and Charles Lindbergh (1902–1974) compare their individual accomplishments in the field of aviation.

17. George S. Patton (1885–1945) and Julius Caesar (100–44 B.C.) acknowledge each other's strengths and weaknesses.

18. William Shakespeare (1564–1616) questions Cleopatra (69–30 B.C.) about her relationship with Mark Antony.

19. Harriet Beecher Stowe (1811–1896) and Mother Teresa (1910–1997) discuss the subject of human dignity.

20. Samuel Morse (1791–1872) and Alexander Graham Bell (1847–1922) praise each other for their accomplishments in the field of global communication.

21. Elizabeth Cady Stanton (1815–1902) and Rosa Parks (1913–2005) share their experiences as social activists.

22. Billie Holiday (1915–1959) and Scott Joplin (1868–1917) plan a concert together.

23. Eleanor Roosevelt (1884–1962) offers Jacqueline Kennedy Onassis (1929–1994) advice on how to raise children in the White House.

24. Sigmund Freud (1856–1939) psychoanalyzes Vincent van Gogh (1853–1890).

25. Hippocrates (460–370 B.C.) and Florence Nightingale (1820–1910) care for a patient together.

26. Julia Child (1912–2004) prepares a meal for Louis XIV of France (1638–1715).

27. Frederick Douglass (1818–1895) and Medgar Evers (1925–1963) thank each other for their efforts to abolish social injustice and racial inequality in America.

28. Babe Ruth (1895–1948) and Jackie Robinson (1919–1972) discuss the changes in baseball since they were players.

29. Thomas Edison (1847–1931) and Alfred Nobel (1833–1896) discuss the value of perseverance.

30. Lady Godiva (980–1067) and Henry Ford (1863–1947) go for a drive together.

31. Napoleon Bonaparte (1769–1821) and Charlemagne (c. 742–814) plan a military invasion together.

32. Henry VIII of England (1491–1547) proposes marriage to Jane Austen (1775–1817).

33. Karl Marx (1818–1883) and Ronald Reagan (1911–2004) discuss their philosophical and economic beliefs.

34. Egyptian Pharaoh Khafre (2520–2494 B.C.) asks Frank Lloyd Wright (1867–1959) for his opinion on the design of the Sphinx.

35. Julius Rosenberg (1918–1953) and Mata Hari (1876–1917) reflect on their lives as accused spies.

36. Sir Isaac Newton (1643–1727) and Albert Einstein (1879–1955) compliment each other for their accomplishments in the fields of math and science.

37. John Lennon (1940–1980) and Robert Johnson (1911–1938) write a song together.

38. Yves Saint Laurent (1936–2008) presents Mary, Queen of Scots (1542–1587) with a dress he designed for her.

39. Henry David Thoreau (1817–1862) encourages John D. Rockefeller (1839–1937) to give up his wealth and simplify his life.

40. Mark Twain (1835–1910) and Richard Pryor (1940–2005) prepare a comic monologue together.

41. Yuri Gagarin (1934–1968) and Sally Ride (1951–2012) reminisce about their adventures in space.

42. Joan of Arc (1412–1431) and Nelson Mandela (1918–2013) recall how they each found the strength to fight for their beliefs.

43. Aristotle (384–322 B.C.) and Albert Camus (1913–1960) contemplate the meaning of life.

44. John Jay (1745–1829) and Thurgood Marshall (1908–1993) share their opinions on justice and equality in America today.

45. Marco Polo (1254–1324) and Leif Eriksson (c. 970–1020) go exploring together.

46. John Dillinger (1903–1934) and Jesse James (1847–1882) plan a bank heist.

47. Indira Gandhi (1917–1984) and Margaret Thatcher (1925–2013) discuss the problems they faced while serving as the first female prime ministers of their respective countries.

48. Isadora Duncan (1877–1927) and Fred Astaire (1899–1987) choreograph a dance together.

49. Johannes Gutenberg (c. 1395–1468) and Benjamin Franklin (1706–1790) consider ideas for a new invention.

50. Ansel Adams (1902–1984) photographs the American frontier while on an expedition with Daniel Boone (1734–1820).

USING IMPROVISATION IN NON-THEATER CLASSES

The benefits of improvisation are not exclusive to theater students. Teachers of all subjects can use improvisation to engage and actively involve students in their learning. Content-specific lessons and concepts can be brought to life in an improvised performance, and improvisation can serve as an interactive assessment tool. Finally, improvisation can help all students build self-confidence, solve problems, think critically and creatively, develop strong interpersonal skills, reduce social anxiety, speak clearly, and listen effectively.

A list of subject-specific improvisation scenarios is included below. Initially, some students might feel self-conscious about participating in an improvisation. Use these tips to run improvisations with students who have limited performance experience:

- Participate in the first few improvisations yourself. Ask for a volunteer to be your partner. If no one volunteers, select one of your more outgoing students. Continue by asking for volunteers. Most students will want to participate once they see how fun it is! If most of your students are highly motivated, then pick names out of a hat.

- Provide some basic instruction on playing to an audience (e.g., projecting, positioning, movement).

- Set a time limit for each improvisation. You'll find that some students can go on forever, while some have little more to say or do after a few seconds. Set a timer for one or two minutes or any amount of time you think is appropriate for your group.

If you find the improvisation has stalled before time is up, end it yourself and either provide another situation or move on to the next players.

- Offer some positive feedback after each performance as encouragement for your players. You may also ask for some feedback from your class.

Business Education

1. After teaching a lesson on entrepreneurship, have your students play young entrepreneurs discussing the challenges they faced when they began their businesses. Students may choose the type of business themselves, or you can offer suggestions.

2. Randomly assign students some commonly used business terms (e.g., accounts payable, cash flow, equity, net worth, return on investment), and have them play business executives using the terms in a corporate meeting. Have your students plan an agenda that would require the use of the terms during their discussions.

3. Give your students tips on effective interviewing strategies, and have your students play interviewers and job applicants for specific occupations. As an added challenge, assign specific personality traits to the interviewers and applicants, and observe how they interact with each other. Allow students to switch roles so everyone gets a chance to play both interviewer and interviewee.

4. Require each student to research a famous person in business (living or dead). Improvise scenes where you play a newspaper reporter interviewing your students as the businesspeople they've researched. You could also have other students in the class take turns playing the reporter instead of you.

5. After a lesson on résumé writing, have students play prospective applicants for different jobs who are helping each other write

their résumés. Provide students with a list of power verbs to use during the improvisation. You can also have your students perform solo improvisations as employers critiquing résumés.

Communications

1. Discuss with your class the qualities of effective public speaking, and then have your students give extemporaneous speeches on random topics. Write the topics on slips of paper, and have each student choose one before speaking.

2. Place your students in pairs, and have them improvise conversations with each other while intentionally using poor speaking characteristics, such as no eye contact or limited vocal variety. Ask the class to identify the ineffective speaking qualities after each scene. Then have the same students perform the conversation using effective speaking qualities.

3. Have two students improvise an argument about something. You may give them a subject to argue about, or they may choose their own. After the improvisation, ask the class to determine which student's argument was the strongest.

4. Have two or more students use a recording of instrumental music as background music for an improvised scene. The students may establish their own characters, situation, and setting, but their visible and vocal expressions should parallel the mood of the music. Follow each improvisation with a class discussion about the effect the music had on the performance.

5. Have students improvise scenes playing candidates for office who are trying to persuade voters to support them. After each scene, ask the class to identify the persuasive techniques used by the candidates. You may wish to review Aristotle's modes of persuasion (ethos, pathos, and logos) before beginning.

English

1. Have your students improvise scenes that include characters from the novels you've assigned in class. Rather than simply reproducing scenes already included in the novel, your students should invent situations that could have logically taken place before or after scenes from the novel. As an added challenge, try mixing characters from different novels.

2. Give your students a list of vocabulary words, and have them improvise conversations with each other using words from the list. As an added twist, tell the students to purposely use some of the words incorrectly and ask the class to try to identify them.

3. Read critical reviews of novels you've assigned to your class, and have your students play those novels' authors responding to the opinions expressed in the reviews. Try to find reviews that include both positive and negative assessments.

4. Have your students play film directors discussing motivations and objectives with actors who are playing characters from the novels. As an alternative, have them improvise scenes as casting agents auditioning actors for various roles.

5. After studying a scene from a play, have your students improvise offstage action that might logically precede or follow the scene. After each performance, ask the class if they thought the action made sense based on their understanding of the situation and characters.

Family and Consumer Science

1. Give students different types of fabrics, and have them improvise scenes as clothing designers who are developing new uses for the materials.

2. Describe an interior setting of a specific room in an empty house, and have your students play interior designers or decorators who've been asked to paint, decorate, and furnish the room.

3. Assign pairs of students the roles of a young child and an adult caretaker. Have them improvise scenes where the child and caretaker meet for the first time. As an added challenge, assign specific behavioral issues to the child, and ask the class to observe how the caretaker deals with those issues.

4. Prepare a list of food items for students to use in an improvisation as cooks who must come up with a recipe using only those ingredients.

5. Distribute copies of restaurant menus to your students, and have them play diners reading the menu and discussing the nutritional content of various selections before placing their orders.

Fine Art

1. Display a painting (or a print of a painting), and have a pair of students pretend to be art critics discussing the painting. For added interest, require one critic to love everything about the painting and the other to hate everything about it.

2. After a lesson on camera operation and control, have your students play photographers discussing which camera settings to choose for specific types of photo shoots.

3. Set up a mini art-and-craft show in your performance area, and have students play visitors at the show who are commenting on the various pieces on display. You may also have students play artisans discussing their work with the visitors.

4. Have your students personify painting and drawing tools (e.g., brushes, pencils, charcoal sticks) who discuss their specific uses with each other. (See chapter seven, "Unreal Improvisations.")

5. Have your students research famous artists and then improvise scenes where they compare each other's concepts and techniques. (See chapter eight, "Historically Speaking.")

Health and Physical Education

1. Have your students improvise allegorical scenes where they play characters with names such as "Stress," "Nutrition," "Exercise," "Disease," "Personal Safety," etc., who discuss their personal characteristics and the effects they have on one another.

2. Have your students research famous athletes and then improvise scenes where they discuss their accomplishments with each other. (See chapter eight, "Historically Speaking.")

3. Have your students personify items commonly found in a gym (e.g., barbells, yoga mats, exercise balls) who discuss with each other their specific uses. (See chapter seven, "Unreal Improvisations.")

4. Select students who excel in different sports, and have them improvise discussions with each other about the specific skills or type of training and conditioning needed for their individual sports.

5. Have students improvise scenes in which they exhibit the physical symptoms of a specific disease, and then ask the class to try to identify the affliction.

Mathematics

1. Have your students improvise activities that involve the use of mathematics (e.g., a cook adjusting a recipe so that it serves three instead of four).

2. Think of various occupations that require mathematical skill, (e.g., economist, stockbroker, tax examiner, accountant, financial planner, engineer). Have your students improvise scenes where they use math skills at work.

3. Have your students personify various types of numbers who discuss their differences with each other (e.g., rational and irrational numbers, odd and even numbers, prime and composite numbers). (See chapter seven, "Unreal Improvisations.")

4. Have your students play famous mathematicians who discuss their contributions to the study of mathematics with each other (e.g., Pythagoras and Euclid discussing their theorems). (See chapter eight, "Historically Speaking.")

5. After teaching a lesson on new ways to solve math problems, have your students play parents questioning their children about the new methods they've learned.

Music

1. Place a number of different musical instruments on a table, and have your students play salespersons in a music store who are helping customers choose instruments to learn.

2. Have your students personify different types of notes (e.g., quarter notes, half notes, whole notes) and other music notation symbols (e.g., rests, fermatas, treble clefs, bass clefs) discussing their value and purpose on a musical staff. (See chapter seven, "Unreal Improvisations.")

3. Assign students roles to play in a rock band (e.g., singer, guitarist, drummer, bassist, keyboard player), and have them improvise a band meeting where they discuss plans to secure a recording contract.

4. Have your students play famous musicians from different eras who are discussing their styles and techniques with each other. (See chapter eight, "Historically Speaking.")

5. Have your students play radio personalities commenting on songs after they play them.

Science

1. Give students some time to research facts about different animals, and have them personify the animals they've researched. (See chapter seven, "Unreal Improvisations.")

2. Have your students play famous scientists (living or dead) discussing the contributions they've made to their individual fields. (See chapter eight, "Historically Speaking.")

3. Have your students personify different elements from the Periodic Table of Elements and discuss with each other their uses and unique properties. They might also discuss what they could do if they got together (e.g., Oxygen and Hydrogen discuss the idea of getting together to become water). (See chapter seven, "Unreal Improvisations.")

4. Have your students improvise conversations with each other in which they discuss the different ways science has improved or simplified their lives.

5. Have your students improvise a scene showing how a specific activity was more difficult to do *before* a certain scientific discovery was made, and then have them perform another scene as older people performing the same activity *after* the discovery was made (e.g., lighting a room before and after electricity was utilized).

Social Studies

1. Have your students play influential historical figures discussing the impact they've made on culture and society. (See chapter eight, "Historically Speaking.")

2. Have students improvise scenes showing people of diverse backgrounds and cultures adapting to unfamiliar environments.

3. Have each student in the class take turns playing the role of a politician speaking at a town-hall meeting. The rest of the class should play the roles of the attendees. You may assign each student a topic for discussion or give each a choice. The meeting should include a question-and-answer period.

4. Have your students reenact current news stories. Other students can play TV news reporters "live" on the scene.

5. Give your students a proposal for a bill, either fictional or real, and have your students play legislators discussing the bill's merits.

Technology Education

1. After reviewing the characteristics of a good website with your students, have them play website designers and business owners who design company websites.

2. Have your students play the roles of students and teachers debating the merits of E-Learning.

3. After a class discussion on the future of technology, have your students play time travelers who've traveled to the future to learn about technological advancements.

4. Have your students play grandparents talking to their grandchildren about what the world was like before smartphones, computers, and other gadgets.

5. Think of activities that would be easier to do if the technology existed, and have your students improvise scenes that show people involved in those activities using futuristic technology.

World Languages

1. Assign each student an inanimate object to personify, and place them in a situation and setting. Choose objects that have cultural significance in a country or place where the language you teach is the primary one. (See chapter seven, "Unreal Improvisations.")

2. Assign each student a partner. Have one student play an American visiting the other student, who plays a cousin living in another country. Place them in a setting where they can observe and discuss similarities and differences between their respective cultures (e.g., a restaurant, a sporting event, a school).

3. After showing a film produced in a country where the language you teach is the primary one, assign each of your students a character from the film and have them improvise off-camera action or a scene that might take place after the film's ending.

4. After teaching lessons on famous world figures (leaders, writers, artists, sports figures, entertainers, etc.) from regions where the language you teach is spoken, assign each of your students a particular person to play and place them in a situation. The figures can be historical or contemporary, living or dead, fictional or nonfictional. For an added twist, assign figures that did not live during the same time period yet have something in common (e.g., French writers Balzac and Camus). (See chapter eight, "Historically Speaking.")

5. Place your students in a specific setting, and have them improvise a discussion that would logically take place in that environment. This would be a good improvisation to run after teaching a lesson on a specific place in a country where the language you teach is the primary one.

INDEX